DIVINING
ANCIENT SITES

– INSIGHTS INTO THEIR CREATION

In loving memory of my late father Dennis Wheatley.

Dedicated to Guy Underwood who discovered the geodetic
system of earth energies and to Raven Wheatley-Hawkins.

Thank you to Patricia and Ray Cox for their editing, contributions and time.
And a special thank you to Busty Taylor and David Webb.

Book design and layout Robert Marron.

Front cover by Hans Messerschmidt

Published by Celestial Songs Press,
66 Cherry Orchard, Marlborough,
Wiltshire. SN8 4AF.

www.theaveburyexperience.co.uk
Email: mariawheatley@aol.com
Telephone 01672 511427.

A CIP record for this book is available from the British Library.

ISBN 978-0-9560733-4-1

CONTENTS

❧

❧

❧

DIVINING
ANCIENT SITES

– INSIGHTS INTO THEIR CREATION

Introduction

❧

Ancient civilizations recognized that the Earth emits harmonic energy. Pyramids, stone circles and temples marked these special locations creating a striking beauty and terrestrial harmony. Separated by thousands of miles, monumental sites were connected by magnetic lines of force streaming over the surface of the Earth with smaller lines that branch off like veins flowing into the countryside. Imbuing the site with unseen power, the direction and strength of the earth energy flow was once measured and modified to suit the needs of the landscape and its people. Connecting terrestrial energies to celestial influences, ancient sites create a bridge between heaven and Earth, man and cosmos.

A hundred and fifty years ago the practice of Feng Shui became known in the West. During the Industrial Revolution European businessmen eager to invest in both China and Hong Kong instantly met opposition, which defied commercial sense. Railways, factories and well-planned straight roads linking important industrial complexes were refused building permits. The reasons given were incomprehensible to their logical Western mindset. They were told that a certain hill range represents the Mercurial Dragon and that no cutting though the hill would be allowed. Straight tracks of railways were likewise rebuffed, as the Chi energy of the land would drain as a consequence. In old China the practice of Feng Shui, meaning 'wind and water – that which cannot be seen and cannot be grasped' - gave the land a quality of beauty and order far beyond the achievement of a Western planner. To Christian missionaries Chinese temples were 'alive' and full of energy that touched the heart and soul of all who entered. In contrast their newly-built chapels and churches felt empty, as if lacking a vital ingredient. This was because prehistoric temple and town development was based not on secular planning but on a sublime metaphysical system in which astronomy, geomancy, science and magic united.

This book reveals the awe-inspiring esoteric knowledge of our ancestors who recognized that the Earth emits mysterious energy patterns. Separated only by time, we too can learn to 'read' and divine the land upon which we live, as did our ancestors. Recognizing and interacting with earth energies is a rewarding experience as Gaia's subtle forces flow like magnetic rivers across the globe. Rivers refresh and cleanse, and, likewise, we can bathe in these magnetic currents to replenish our energy levels and raise our consciousness. Ancient peoples worldwide identified healing earth patterns and utilized their emissions by placing temples and their dwellings upon them. In the same way we too can benefit from this energetic eco system which brings longevity and a sense of well-being to our lives.

Using simple dowsing instruments we will locate earth energies and leys and observe how they influence sacred sites, our homes and workspaces, and you will witness first hand how they can dramatically affect the scintillating colours of the aura. To further our understanding of the Earth we will investigate how geodetic lines and their geometric patterns can create magical spaces where we can commune with Gaia, or receive healing.

We shall also discover how to negate inharmonious earth energies using colour healing and how to make harmonic healing remedies.

Where we were born may seem irrelevant to our adult lives, yet the moment we incarnated we unconsciously created a two way magnetic umbilical cord to the Earth, which is called a 'vivaxis'. Pioneers of vivaxis treatments have noted that if we align and clear our vivaxis health and well-being can be maintained. A strengthened alignment corrects any imbalances, abnormal nerve or muscle disorders and destroys foreign bodies such as bacteria or viruses. Simple exercises show you how to align to your vivaxis to optimize your physical health and to develop a deep connection to the Earth.

To ancient people the Earth was sacred and was the mother of all things. For millennia humankind believed that in the Earth dwelt the 'soul substance' and that from the Earth came the spirit which gives life to all things, and at death returned to it. Earth energies were regarded as a manifestation of this life spirit. Earth's life force was known to numerous ancient societies; to the Sioux

Nations of North America it was known as Wakonda and to the Australian Aborigines it was called Arungquiltha. The ancient Chinese referred to it as Chi and ling and developed a geomantic science to explain it. Throughout the ancient world this universal knowledge was applied to all temple structures creating a global energetic system beating in harmony with the Earth's pulse.

I am a second-generation dowser. I have spent half my life interacting with earth energies and I want to share my knowledge and love of the Earth with you. My late father, Dennis Wheatley, was considered one of Britain's top Master Dowsers and he decoded numerous ancient sites and Templar churches. He was given the unpublished manuscripts and surveys of the field archaeologist and Master Dowser Guy Underwood (1883–1964). During the 1940s – 1960s Guy surveyed numerous sacred sites in the UK and Europe and he rediscovered the *geodetic system of earth energies*. He concluded that geodetic energies were skilfully integrated into the foundation plans of ancient sites creating a lasting connection to a global energy system. Our research shows that when a standing stone or construct is sited upon a geodetic energy pattern or line it becomes spiritually alive rippling with harmonic sine wave energy. Everything that was sited on the geodetic energy system became interconnected creating a unified global energy matrix which was undoubtedly harnessed and dispersed. We openly share over 80 years of research with you and present a new breathtaking vision of how to live in harmony with the Earth.

Standing stones and constructs sited above a powerful geospiral pattern are imbued with healing earth energy. Legend says that if a child suffering from rickets is passed through a Long Stone hole it will be cured. Certainly cured my bad knee.

CHAPTER 1
Sacred water, healing energies

The Earth is a living being and she is over four billion years old. Her immense age and deep understanding of the cycles of time can impart incredible wisdom to us. The Earth, like us, has a physical body which we can see, smell, taste and touch. She also has an invisible subtle body which can be likened to our auric and chakra system. The human subtle body has other vital systems: a network of interconnecting energy channels called meridians or 'nadis' (the word nad means to flow). We have a number of major channels – meridians – and a vast number of increasingly finer minor ones. Similarly, the Earth has major and minor meridian lines or leys which are intimately associated with vital energy centres – chakras – where earth energy converges and emerges. At these locations the Earth emits distinctive geometric patterns which are beneficial to all living organisms.

The idea that some spots upon the Earth were better than others for people to live upon is millennia old. The ancient Chinese were the first to document how to locate and interpret such places. Written texts over 4,000 years old describe powerful currents of earth energy that run invisibly over the planet. Chinese Feng Shui Masters refer to these energies as 'lung mei', the 'dragon's breath', which is also called Chi. In imperial times these energetic and mystical pathways were directed by a government bureau, the Board of Rites. The practitioner of Feng Shui saw Chi manifested in the landscape as opposing and harmonizing influences (yin/yang) which generate an omnidirectional vital force called *ling¹* – spirit – a living universal energy. Ling is shapeless, tasteless, odourless and shadowless but, like air currents, it can be felt on contact. The Chinese Board of Rites strictly regulated the siting and architecture of houses and temples, roads and tombs and so on. Identifying ling-energy which, as we shall see, 'follows the descending ridges of mountains which rise towards heaven and other edifices', was at the heart of Feng Shui. Chi moves within the

Earth's crust in constantly changing spirals which promotes harmony, longevity, prosperity and abundance. Our forefathers realized that these energies can be identified, collected or dispersed, increased or diminished by the nature of the construct sited there.

The Earth's living energy manifests in particular ways and is therefore easy to identify. By recognising the harmonic patterns and lines of force that the Earth emits we can interpret the hidden characteristics of the land. By doing so we can explain why a location or a house has a foreboding or an uplifting atmosphere. For centuries Master Masons and esoteric architects have located these powerful earth patterns which dictated the position of their constructs.

Holy water, sacred patterns

In *The Essential Dowsing Guide* we briefly looked at the geospiral pattern. We will now explore in detail its esoteric secrets and powerful healing properties. To ancient peoples the esoteric centre or 'navel' of the land was a powerful concept. The centre of the land was the focal point of its sacred energy, the place where the soul or genii of the locale resided. In ancient China Peking was placed at the centre of the Chinese landscape in the same way that an English manor house or stately home stands at the centre of its landscape. Throughout the ancient world the geospiral pattern marked the esoteric centre of a temple, stone circle or pyramid. Constantly emitting harmonious energy it imbues the site or building with life-enhancing energy. Generated by a particular type of underground water the geospiral pattern was revered throughout the ancient world. Geodetic dowsers consider it the most powerful form of earth energy which we have studied for over 20 years.

Sacred Yin water

I was taught a little-known truth about water which I want to impart: there are two types of water. Geologists correctly inform us that rain water fills up the water table, aquifers, lakes, rivers and reservoirs and we are all familiar with this type of water. However, there is another type of water called *primary water* (often referred to as a blind spring) which can be found in large quantities beneath the earth. During the 1940s the Master Dowser and field archaeologist Guy Underwood discovered that a blind spring manifests a distinctive harmonic surface pattern which he called a geospiral. To the mystic, primary water is alive, feminine, healing and sacred. I call this water yin water as it is produced chemically deep within the Earth and it is completely independent of rainfall (yang water). Internally the Earth continually produces primary water, and so a blind spring will never run dry. Pressure forces the yin water upwards through vertical fault lines and when it eventually reaches the surface it is revered as a 'sacred spring'. Holy wells renowned for their medicinal properties are invariably sited above the geospiral pattern indicating a prominent source of yin water. As we shall soon see, yang water emits a distinctive pattern and an inharmonious energy field. Long-term exposure to this field is injurious to health, whereas 'yin' water emits a harmonic healing field. Both types of water are safe to drink.

The Geospiral pattern

Yin water emits a geospiral which is a geometrically perfect spiral with coils in multiples of 3½, 7, 14, 21, 28, 35, 42 and 49. These geodetic centres can be likened to chakra points, the 3½-coiled geospiral represents the base chakra and the 7-coiled geospiral represents the heart chakra. Two energy flows called a 'necklace' are located a short distance from the coils. Necklaces have several gaps which allow energy lines to free-flow through it. The smaller 'S' shape spiral orientates itself on the most powerful energy line in the vicinity.

All healing

Animals are instinctively attracted to the geospiral pattern. Farmers have noted that animals kept in enclosed spaces frequently attempted to break out when they are about to give birth. Underwood dowsed numerous birthing locations and found they were sited upon, or in close proximity to, a geospiral. Animals would not behave in this manner unless it was of advantage to them. Further observations revealed that the geospiral appeared to ease labour and produced healthier offspring. After several years of research Underwood concluded that the geospiral had health-giving and restorative properties which are instinctively recognized by animals. Cows, sheep and horses often stand or sleep above a geospiral pattern.

Additional supporting evidence for the geospiral's healing properties came from anecdotal reports from World War II veterans. Whilst on manoeuvres and sleeping rough soldiers noted that if they slept where a cow had previously lain they would wake up feeling healthier and with no rheumatic discomfort. The notion that some auspicious quality attaches to a place where a cow lies down to rest is of great antiquity. Thebes was founded by Cadmus where a sacred cow came to rest. The site of Troy was similarly selected by Ilius and legends say Antioch was built over the place where Io died after she had been transformed into a white cow by the god Zeus.

H20 and H302

Scientific evidence supports the concept of yin water's therapeutic properties. Dr. Gerald Pollack is one of the leading research scientists in the world when it comes to understanding the physics of water and what it means to your health. He is a professor of bioengineering at the University of Washington and the founder and editor of a scientific journal called *Water*. His seminal book, *The Fourth Phase of Water: Beyond Solid, Liquid, and Vapor*, challenges the way we think about water.

Gilbert Ling is also a pioneer in this field. He discovered that water in human cells is not ordinary water (H2O) but something far more structured, which is called the 'fourth phase of water', also known as 'exclusion zone water' or 'EZ' water. EZ water appears in great abundance within your body including inside most of your cells. Other inherent differences between regular water and EZ water include its structure. For instance, tap water is H2O but this fourth phase water is not H2O; it's actually H3O2. It's also more viscous, more ordered and more alkaline than regular water, and its optical properties are different.

Dr Pollack informs us that: *EZ water is alkaline and carries a negative charge.*

Maintaining this state of alkalinity and negative charge appears to be important for optimal health. A natural source of EZ water for drinking is glacial melt. Another good source is water from deep sources such as deep spring water. The deeper the better, as EZ water is created under pressure.

Yin water comes from a deep source, is created under pressure and is therefore an excellent source of EZ water. It is easily identifiable by its geospiral pattern. I suggest deep yin water is H302 water and this is why throughout history it has been regarded as healing. Simply put modern day science is confirming ancient water divining lore!

Body water

My own research into the healing properties of the geospiral reveals how to make the most of its therapeutic power. The Earth's inner waters can cleanse our own body water – and the experience is truly profound. Our bodies are made up of 75% water; likewise, Earth's oceans cover about 75% of the planet and the inner bodies of underground water are vast.

According to the authors Pia Smith Orleans and Cullen Baird Smith who wrote *Conversations with Laarkmaa – A Pleiadian View of a New Reality*, (Auhtorhouse 2010), water is magic. I had the privilege of meeting them at Avebury Henge. Pia and Cullen channel Pleiadian teachings from Laarkmaa to assist humankind's evolution. One of their teachings concerns water and is parallel to our own understanding of its esoteric properties. 'Humans tend to think of themselves as static, unchanging, and solid which we are not; we are fluid', says Laarkmaa. 'Body water is directly influenced by surface water and underground water, both of which can reactivate our DNA, and also heal us. Our DNA is a pool of material like water; it is not layered linearly'.

Within the geospiral's magnetic spiral field our own body water can be cleansed and rejuvenated. All water has memory; this is a fundamental principle of holistic practices such as homeopathy. Similarly, I believe that our body water can record and memorize information and can hold onto painful memories. By cleansing our body water we can release unwanted memories, outmoded behaviours, attitudes and even dis-ease.

Cleansing your body water

When we consciously work with Earth's inner waters a channel is created and remarkable changes occur. The following meditation has been developed for group or individual work which gently arouses the geospiral's light energy which passes through and cleanses the body's chakra system. Because you are working with the Earth's planetary body it is more powerful than concentrating in isolation on your own chakras. If you use this visualization technique on a regular basis it will keep your body water cleansed and your energy centres refreshed and balanced. Often during meditation light is called down from 'above' and the energy seems to be 'outside' the individual, but in this technique the light is inherent within the Earth's inner being which interacts with your inner being. Incidentally, Earth's inner light often manifests externally as an 'earthlight' – a glowing ball of white or amber light. (Often referred to as a ball of light or 'BOL', or light plasma.)

This technique is more effective whilst standing upon a geospiral, although it may also be done sat down cross-legged. Earth energy patterns are geophysical arenas in which consciousness can be changed.

- Standing with your arms by your side take several deep breaths until your breathing becomes soft, deep and regular. If sitting touch the ground with your hands. Smile and enjoy the energies of where you are.

- Ask Mother Earth to protect and guide you throughout this meditation.

- Visualize, or sense, the geospiral beneath your feet and around you.

- Become aware of the sacred point of contact between you and the Earth.

- Now visualize or sense a source of energy just below the ground emanating from the geospiral. This is usually felt as a 'warm' or tingling feeling and can be seen or sensed as a golden energy light sphere – an earthlight. The upper surface of this golden sphere touches the soles of your feet (or buttocks/legs if sitting cross-legged), and from its lower surface a beautiful strand of light descends into the land and soon becomes anchored into the earth. This wonderful golden earthlight is going to cleanse your being, wash away painful memories, remove any unwanted influences or heal a particular area of the physical body. Ask the deep inner waters what you require and set your intent: healing, cleansing, rejuvenation, etc.

- Now increase your awareness of the golden earthlight beneath your feet – you may feel a sensation of heat where your feet touch the ground.

- In a moment we are going to use breathing to draw the earth's energy into our being.

Druid Wisdom

According to Celtic author R.J. Stewart, and several Druid authorities, there are four major centres in the body which represent the four elements that reflect the Inner and Outer World of Gaia. These are the Feet, Base chakra, Heart chakra,

Head – throat, third eye and crown chakras. We are going to work with the Four Elements to assist the cleansing and healing process.

- **Feet – Earth Star Chakra – Element of Earth –** Become aware that you are standing on the Earth's body and become aware of your own body. Take a slow deep breath and feel the golden earthlight rise up through the soles of your feet (which are minor chakras) and into your ankles, calves, thighs and hips. As the light ascends it fills your body with beautiful light which cleanses and purifies your body water. This is the first stage of energy cleansing.

- **Base Chakra – Element of Water –** As the earthlight ascends to the base chakra area become aware of the Earth's inner water and the waters of your own body. Honour the waters of the world, honour your own water. Water is a fundamental element of your cells, it is the element required for creation and birth. Visualize, or simply sense, the golden earthlight cleansing your base chakra area. This is the second stage of energy cleansing.

- **Heart Chakra – Element of Fire –** As the earthlight sphere moves upwards through the body it momentarily stops in the navel and solar plexus areas, cleansing and balancing as it moves. As the sphere rises through your body it becomes brighter symbolizing the element of fire which illuminates your heart chakra; and cleanses this beautiful centre. At this stage, if you have a painful memory or an emotional issue you would like to transform, picture it in your minds eye and let it gently fall into the earthlight sphere, into the cleansing light. If healing is required ask Gaia's light to heal the selected area and see it illuminated with radiant light right down to the cellular level. This is the third stage of energy cleansing.

- **Head – Throat, Third Eye, and Crown Chakras – Element of Air –** As the earthlight sphere moves upwards through the body it momentarily stops midway between the heart and throat area, which is called the *Universal Heart* or *8th Chakra²*. Allow the light to ascend to the throat area, cleansing and balancing this chakra. Now, let the earthlight rise once more to cleanse and harmonize the Third Eye, so that your intuitive sight will be clear and radiant. This is the fourth stage of energy cleansing. The earthlight ascends once more to just above your head symbolizing that you are a child of heaven as well as of the Earth. You are clear and radiant filled with the resplendent light of Mother Earth.

- **Returning Gaia's Power –** When you feel ready slowly return Gaia's light by reversing the process. Let the earthlight sphere slowly descend though the chakras, through your feet, into the heart of the land and into the deep internal waters from whence it came.

- Thank Gaia.

Locating geospirals

Experience geospiral energy at the centres of most ancient sites, such as stone circles, long barrows, Celtic brochs, cairns, Irish round towers, dolmens, medicine wheels and man-made mounds or pyramids. Solitary standing stones also mark geospiral energy. Geospirals are also found at the altars or fonts of old medieval churches in Ireland, England and Scotland.

Only a small proportion of Native American earthworks that once marked sacred energy centres have survived the passage of time. A serpentine earthwork that artistically displays awareness of the geospiral phenomenon was recorded in 1858. Just a few centuries ago this earthen wonder spiralled around the landscape of the Blue Earth river, Iowa.

Interacting and dowsing geospirals

- Stand at the near centre of a sacred site.
- With a single rod – or a pair of dowsing rods – in 'search' (pointing straight ahead and parallel to the ground) visualize the geospiral pattern in the earth beneath the ground. Attune to the geospiral.
- Silently command the rod/s to *show you the coils of the geospiral pattern*.
- Repeating this command in your mind make a slow, straight dowsing pass walking straight ahead. The rod/s will swing into the 'found' position when a coil had been detected.
- Reset the rod/s to 'search' upon detecting each coil. Geospirals vary from around 10 to 100 paces. Now locate the necklace by tuning into the pattern.

Finding geospirals in the landscape

- If you do not live near a sacred site you can find a geospiral in the open countryside. First, using information dowsing you need to establish if there is a geospiral pattern within, say, 50 or 100 feet (15.24 or 30.48 metres) of where you are standing. If the rod/s answer is 'yes' gently command your dowsing instrument to *show you the direction of the nearest geospiral.* The rod will waver and eventually point to a particular direction. Align yourself to that direction and walk slowly forwards until the rod swings into the 'found' position. You have located the spiral pattern. Alternatively, map dowse for a geospiral using the 'two point fix' explained in *The Essential Dowsing Guide.*

Lunar influences

Geospirals are constantly rotating in either a clockwise or an anti-clockwise direction. Master dowsers have noted that two geospirals coexist together, one having a clockwise rotation (yang energy) and the other an anti-clockwise rotation (yin energy). However, one geospiral will 'dominate' and it is this spiral which reacts to dowsing. Six days after a new or full moon a rotational 'switch' occurs, from a clockwise rotation to an anti-clockwise rotation and vice-versa. These particular days in the lunar cycle modify the geodetic system of earth energies. Interestingly, most ancient calendars were lunar and according to the Celtic calendar found at Coligny, France, the months commenced on the sixth day after the new moon, while the years began on the sixth day after the first new moon following the Spring Equinox. The Greek historian, Pliny the Elder (AD 23-79), wrote that the British Druids only gathered mistletoe on the sixth day after a full moon and that the revered Druidic 'snake's egg' could only be collected on the sixth day after a new moon. However, it must be noted that in some latitudes the switch occurs at the first and last quarters, as latitude will effect the day of the rotational switch.

Throughout Roman Europe the badge of office of the Roman pontiffs was the 'lituus' which was a divining rod made from a straight twig and twisted to form a spiral. The principle functions of the pontiffs were to fix the calendar and calculate the dates and times of religious rites and ceremonies. Undoubtedly these historical references show an intimate awareness of the moon's influence upon the geospiral phenomenon.

Yin water, wealth and abundance

In the early 1990s an old Chinese Feng Shui Master, who was a friend and colleague of my late father, informed us that Peking (modern day Beijing) was purposely sited above a vast blind spring. Peking prospered from this placement which generated one of the world's largest geospirals. In Feng Shui terms water represents money and signifies the flow of wealth. Likewise the English term 'currency' is derived from a river's current reflecting the water-money connection. Ancient city planning was based on metaphysical principles and financial institutions, including the City of London's centre, and large banking organizations were placed above yin water that generates the geospiral pattern. Representing movement and the flow of money the inner waters of the Earth ensure a golden harvest to those that understand its esoteric principles.

The old Chinese geomancer taught us well. Many years later it was reported in New Scientist magazine 2007 that two American scientists, Jesse Lawrence of the University of California and Michael E. Wysession of Washington University, using seismic waves located a vast ocean, comparable to the Arctic Ocean beneath Beijing. Geophysict Alan B Thompson's article in *Nature* magazine points out that the mantle of the Earth, the deep layers of rock structures, contains lodes of water, like mineral lodes that dwarf the existing oceans. In other words there is more underground water in the Earth's lower mantle than there is in all the Earth's oceans.

Magical Circles

Power places such as Stonehenge and the Giza pyramids are special locations which are sited above a combination of earth energies that rise to the surface bestowing the site with its own particular geo-signature or *Spirit of Place*. Ancient architects interpreted the geophysical properties of the land, and, likewise, if we can recognize the prevailing earth energies of a given location we 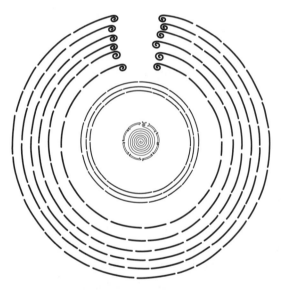 can interpret the land's ambience, character and spiritual purpose. Places where earth energies converge or emerge were especially potent and became regional power centres.

Throughout the ancient world circular structures dominated the landscape. They mark a powerful earth energy pattern which energizes any structure sited upon it. Using a highly sensitive dowsing instrument Underwood noted that an exceptionally strong blind spring generates a threefold energy pattern; the geospiral marks its centre and it is surrounded by a circular and a semicircular energy pattern as shown in the illustration.

Primary haloes

Underwood called the circular energy pattern a *primary halo* and we discovered that it invariably dictates the location, size and shape of prehistoric circular structures, such as stone circles, earthen mounds and medicine wheels. A primary halo consists of three rings of strong magnetic force; however, exceptionally powerful blind springs can generate six rings of energy.

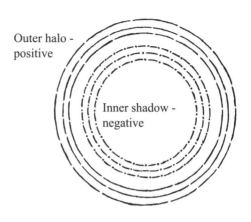

Primary haloes are cut into segments which allow the free flow of energy lines into and out of the area.

Amplifying the energy

Our research shows that primary haloes have extraordinary power and range from several to over a hundred feet (30.48 metres) in diameter. Any structure sited upon it will be perpetually charged with unseen energy. This is because the halo has two remarkable characteristics, a positive outer halo, and a negative inner (or sometimes outer) 'shadow'. Periodically the inner negative 'shadow' will exchange places with the positive outer halo and then revert back to its original position. This perpetual switching motion charges the area with energy. Standing stones sited on the outer halo are continually being energized. The stone's silica crystal lattice absorbs the earth energy and then transmits it in a coherent manner by producing 'energy bands'. A tall standing stone generates seven energy bands, which I liken to megalithic chakra points. The bands spiral within and around the stone and convert the earth energy into a form of aerial energy. Two energy bands are below ground and five are above ground as shown in the illustration. Bands two, four and five release the energy in a linear beam of energy which travels across the landscape in a form of Neolithic WiFi.

Defying physics

Each band functions in a particular manner. Remarkably, one band can change one's body weight by either reducing or gaining weight in a matter of minutes. Our recordings show that a staggering two stone of body weight was mysteriously gained when the palms of the hands were placed firmly against a particular section of the band. When the hands were removed, or placed elsewhere, the body weight instantly returned to normal. Likewise in reverse, my body weight became lighter when the palms of the hands interacted with the nodal point. What is going on? If this anomaly was recognized and manipulated by our ancestors, the band may have assisted in the transportation of heavy stone by reducing the overall weight of the megalith or stone block. We are currently conducting experiments to understand this phenomenon. Alongside Rodney Hale we have detected the bands electromagnetic frequencies which prove their existence and this is explained fully in *Avebury, Sun, Moon, and Earth*, available at www.theaveburyexperience.co.uk.

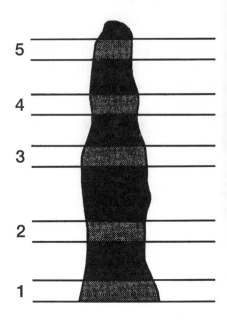

Modern structures and haloes

Haloes have a stimulating effect and prolonged exposure to their energy field is not conducive to good health; however, short-term exposure is energizing and uplifting. One particular London office, which is partially sited on the outer edge of a halo, attracted a highly motivated and hard-working workforce, although many employees were prone to high stress levels caused by overworking. We surveyed the location and noted that the restroom was located directly above the halo making relaxation difficult. Moving the restroom away from the area proved successful; the workforce found they could relax and chill out. This example shows how the interpretation of earth energies can be applied to our modern-day working lives.

Locating a primary halo

You can interact with primary halo energy at most circular sites such as stone circles, Irish and Scottish round towers, medicine wheels and man-made mounds such as Maes Howe, Orkney and some pyramids. American dowsers have informed me that the White House in Washington DC is sited above a powerful geospiral and primary halo pattern.

Interacting and dowsing a halo at a stone circle or medicine wheel

- Tune into the energy by visualizing the primary halo energy pattern in the Earth beneath a circular structure.

- With a single rod, or a pair of rods in 'search', (pointing straight ahead and parallel to the ground) silently command the rod/s to show you a primary halo circle. Repeat this command in your mind and make a slow straight dowsing pass towards the circular structure.

- When the dowsing rod has detected a circle it will swing into the 'found' position.

- Reset the rod/s to 'search'.

- Repeat the procedure until you have found all of the haloes. In a similar manner see if you can detect the inner (or outer) shadow.

Salisbury Cathedral's spire is sited above a geospiral and a large primary halo. Spire and dome shapes encourage earth energy to spiral towards the apex imbuing the building with spiritual energy. The word 'spire' may have been derived from geospiral.

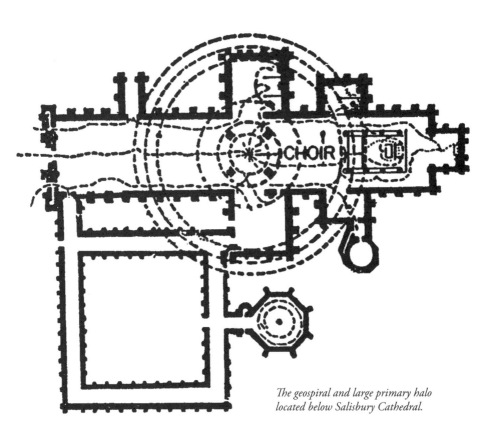

The geospiral and large primary halo located below Salisbury Cathedral.

Secondary haloes

Secondary haloes are only produced by exceptionally powerful blind springs and they are often located hundreds of feet away from the central geospiral. Symbolically when a secondary halo is integrated into a temple or megalithic complex it serves to 'consecrate' and 'protect' the area from unwanted intrusion. Similar to primary haloes, secondary haloes have an outer or inner shadow which energizes the geometry. The energizing process

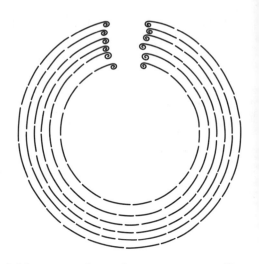

creates an external magnetic force field surrounding the monument. Guy Underwood did little research on this incredible pattern. Our research shows that the semi-circular halo has six flow lines. However, six days after a new moon it may multiply to 12 and six days after a full moon it may multiply to 18 before returning to its original number. The large 'gap' allows powerful energy lines to either enter or leave the monument. The halo was an essential component of monumental planning serving to separate the sacred from the profane outer regions.

Locating a secondary halo

Secondary haloes surround large megalithic complexes and power places. Old walled cities are often sited above a secondary halo decreeing its boundary and protecting the enclosure. Stonehenge has a protective secondary halo making it one of the most accessible sites to dowse. Locate and experience the energy close to the Stonehenge Avenue by simply applying the dowsing technique used for

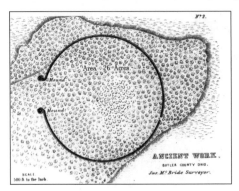

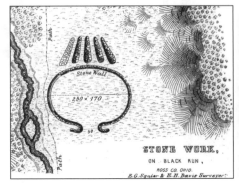

detecting a primary halo. Ancient American sacred sites may have integrated the secondary halo pattern and two examples from Ohio that were surveyed by Ephraim Squier and Edwin Davis are shown. Resembling a secondary halo, the left-hand illustration of an earthen horseshoe close to Hamilton, Butler County, enclosed 16 acres and its entrance was 275 feet (83.32 metres) wide.

Energy Arcs

Energy arcs run from one blind spring to another and only occur above blind springs of exceptional force. Energetically speaking, arcs connect sacred sites to one another and their concave sides usually face inwards towards the direction of the geospiral. Their spiral ends always occur in multiples of three and a half coils, seven 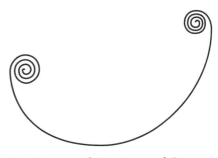 being the commonest. The design of classical columns of Grecian and Roman architecture may have been inspired by this delicate energy pattern.

Endnotes

1. Phenomena Thames and Hudson 1977 p78 John Michell and Robert J.M. Rickard
2. Hope Hay House 2011 Jude Currivan.

15

Arthur's Stone ley, Hay-on-Wye.

The ley begins at Mouse Castle, targets Arthur's Stone, St Michael's and All Saints church at Moccas Court and St Mary's church at Monnington on Wye.

Curiously, sited on private ground close to the ley is a circle of heads on stone pillars resembling the Churchill family and onto St Mary's church at Credenhill.

CHAPTER 2
Leys and ley systems

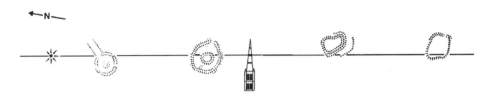

Straight trackways and linear alignments connect ancient sites to one another in a vast system that originated in prehistoric times. During my research I found one of the earliest references to leys documented by Dr John Dee (1527-1606). The Royal astrologer and magician to Queen Elizabeth I wrote: *The true mathematical science is that which measureth the invisible lines and immortal beams which can pass through cold and turf, hill and dale. It was for this reason, it was accounted by all ancient priests the chiefest science; for it gave them power both in their words and works.* However, it was not until 1925 when Alfred Watkins published a book called, *The Old Straight Track* that leys became widely known to the general public. He noticed that straight lines, formed by old tracks and pathways created linear alignments across the countryside, and ancient manmade structures were sited upon them, such as tumuli, long barrows, stone circles, and standing stones. Watkins called these linear alignments 'leys'.

Ley classifications

The phrase ley is a generic term, as there are several different types of leys. Sig Lonegren, the well-known American dowser, recognized this and categorised them into four main groups:

- The ***Topographical ley*** is the traditional Watkins style of linear alignment. It emits no energy and simply connects ancient sites to one another in a linear fashion.

- The ***Energy ley*** emits and transmits energy and it follows invisible lines of force.

- The ***Astronomical ley*** is orientated towards the sun, moon, or a celestial object, and this is supported by the fact that numerous ancient roads and straight tracks follow the course of the sun at ceremonial times of the year.

- The ***Topographical astronomical energy ley*** is especially powerful as it is linear, emits and transmits energy along its course, is associated with several sacred sites, and orientated towards a celestial object, such as the sun at the summer solstice.

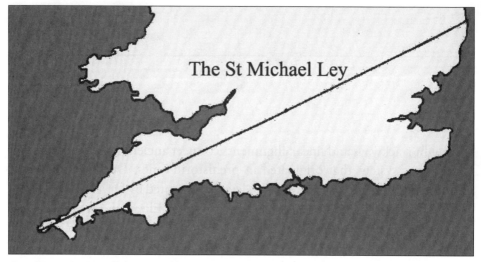

The St Michael Ley

One of Britain's most well documented leys is the St Michael ley, discovered by John Michell. Avebury Henge which contains the world's largest stone circle is sited at its exact centre. It was aligned to the May Day (Beltane) sunrise and the Nov 1 (Samhain) sunset. Author David Furlong calculated its orientation may have been to the setting of the star Mintaka in Orion's belt c2800 BC.

- ***Global leys*** The Iron Age Druids spoke of 'twelve great courts' that encircle the globe. One global ley courses through Stonehenge and the Avebury complex creating a powerful Prime Meridian Line, which was the original Greenwich Meridian line of prehistory.

- ***Ley systems*** Research has shown that some leys form exotic ley systems and two notable examples are described below.

- ***City leys*** Roads that lead to an old city centre through medieval 'gates' are aligned upon leys. The romantic city of Verona, Italy, has a central market square and market cross which marks the crossing point of two powerful leys. The illustration on page 17 shows the old city of Bristol, England, with its High Cross marking a ley crossing which has since been removed to the gardens of Stourhead in Wiltshire.

Leys can course for a short distance or for hundreds of miles; however, the most powerful leys encircle the globe and energetically connect sacred sites worldwide. The geophysical properties of the land will affect the frequency and strength of a ley. Conductive substances such as crystals, underground water, and gold, silver or copper-based minerals lodes will amplify the ley's energy levels within the vicinity. I experienced this in Arkansas, USA. My dowsing response to grid lines was especially strong due to the crystal deposits found beneath the surface. Leys invariably have an energizing influence as energy travels exceptionally fast along a straight line. In Old China, a stone statue, or a large object was placed on the line to slow down its chi force and harmonize its flow.

Ley systems – a celestial planetarium

In the 19th century, long before Watkins rediscovered Britain's ley network, the Rev. Edward Duke described a remarkable ley. Duke was a respected scholar who made several important astronomical discoveries at Stonehenge, many of which are still featured in archaeological books. In 1846 Duke claimed that the majority of ancient sites within thirty miles (48 kilometres) of Stonehenge were sited upon a topographical line. Furthermore, Duke stated that the position of the monuments represented a planetary framework of the solar system. The prehistoric architects had created a planetarium on Earth, with each ancient site representing a particular planet, and its orbital path encircled the countryside. This geocentric viewpoint had Silbury Hill, the largest manmade mound in Europe, as Earth.

Planetary sites

Avebury Henge was associated with the orbital paths of the sun and the moon. The southern inner circle was the temple of the sun and the northern inner circle the temple of the moon. The sun represents the Spirit/Father aspect of

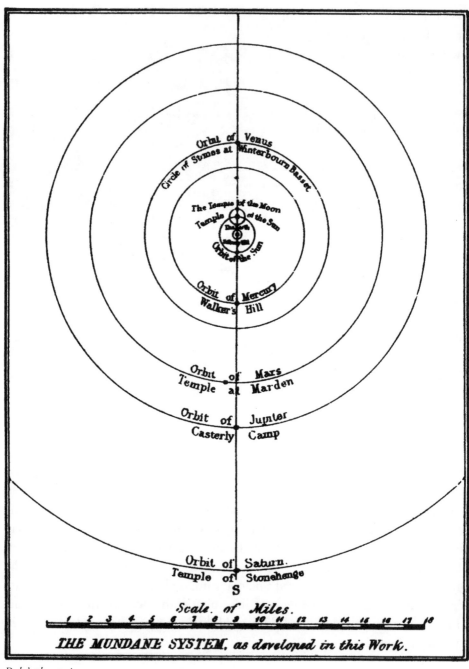

Duke's planetarium

creation and the moon the Soul and Mother. They are our celestial parents and Venus is the daughter of the moon.

Venus

Venus was represented by a concentric stone circle that once stood to the north of Avebury, close to the village of Winterbourne Basset. Duke reported that a standing stone sited to the west of the stone circle was an astronomical marker stone. *For the purpose of directing the astronomical eye of the observer to the declination of this fair orb Venus beneath the apex of the stone.*

Venus's astrological glyph is likened to the Egyptian Ankh meaning *life*. All the kingdoms of life are emanations from Mother Nature and this once beautiful concentric stone circle and its long avenue that coursed to the north would have looked like part of the Ankh. It is tempting to think that an eastern and western avenue or an alignment of single stones once formed the symbol in its entirety. During the 18th century, at the height of the stone smashing holocaust, this temple was one of the first to be destroyed. Local

The only surviving standing stone of the Temple of Venus

people grieved knowing that the heart of the land was sharing their pain as the stone circle was forcibly removed from its birthplace. Only one stone survived which was re-erected relatively recently. Like an immortal guardian it overlooks the site of the vanished stone circle, reminding us of what was once the great Goddess Temple. Although the stones have long gone, an air of majestic feminine power still lingers, like mist upon the land, perceptible but elusive, changing with the moods of the seasons.

Mercury

'Adam's Grave', a 5000-year-old Neolithic long barrow on Walker's Hill, equates with the planet Mercury. Dated to c3800 BC the mound is 200 feet (60 metres) long. Today the large mound is completely grass covered; however, originally a retaining wall of sarsens and dry-stone walling surrounded the barrow. Inside the mound there were megalithic chambers, similar to those at the West Kennet long barrow. Busty Taylor discovered that the mound faces the direction of the midwinter sunrise, and every winter solstice the sun's rays would have illuminated the far chamber. Around 2500 BC the barrow was decommissioned and closed down by Neolithic man by in-filling the inner megalith chambers with earth, sealing it for all time.

Historically, Mercury has been a god of many talents, all of which deal with various aspects of writing, communication, speaking, learning, commerce and message giving. In ancient Egypt, Mercury is Thoth, Lord of Divine Books, and Scribe of the Company of Gods. Adam's Grave is therefore an ideal location to activate the qualities of Mercury, active intelligence, logic, reason, and on a higher level to be the transmitter of the spiritual to the material realms.

Mars

Laser-like the Duke line courses south and targets an ancient Neolithic site called Marden Henge, which corresponds to Mars, although this site is just off the ley. Interestingly, the name of the site reflects its planetary connection, Mar-den, *den* meaning settlement, and therefore the *Settlement of Mars*. Sadly, Marden Henge is but a ruin today but in prehistoric times it was one of the largest henge complexes in Britain (a henge is an enclosed area defined by an inner ditch and an external earthen bank). Recent archaeological excavations have unearthed houses, religious constructs and sweat lodges.

Mars is associated with strong masculine qualities and a war-like nature. Mars gives courage, conviction and the physical energy and stamina to achieve. Mars is said to be the warrior and murderer, but it is also the surgeon and the healer. When the energy of Mars is properly channelled it is the mystic and the servant of Humanity.

Jupiter

Following the line further south we encounter the ancient site of Casterley Camp, the largest Druid ceremonial centre in Wiltshire. It corresponds to the planet Jupiter. Jupiter is the largest planet in the solar system and although its distance from Earth varies between 365 and 600 million miles (587.4 and 965 million kilometres), Jupiter is so huge and luminous that it is easily seen at night with the naked eye. To astrologers it symbolizes wisdom, expansion, spiritual truth and vision. It is said to be the 'great benefactor' and the bestower of material gifts and abundance.

A poetic translation of Casterley Camp is the *Castle on the Ley*. The site, which encloses over 60 acres, was never intended to be a defensive hill fort, as the banks are far too low, although ironically it is now sited on M.o.D. territory. Never enter the site when the military 'red flag' is flying, as this is an impact area. Nonetheless, it was once a magnificent Druid city and no doubt a place of learning – a Druid Cor. The Druid Colleges, or Cors, were renowned throughout Europe as centres of advanced education. Therefore, it should come as no surprise that one of England's most famous universities, the University of Oxford, was sited upon a Druid Cor. The 360-degree horizon line that Casterley Camp offers makes it appear more like an astronomical observatory. In the distance you can see the Alton Barnes White Horse which is sited beneath Adam's Grave long barrow, and it is easy to trace out the Duke line flowing like a mystical pathway though the land.

Nearby is the Enford Barrow, which is the largest earthen mound on

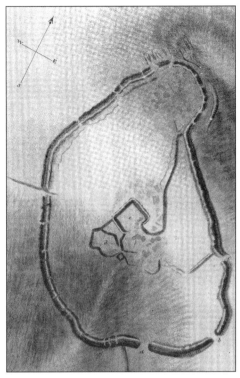

Casterley Camp

Salisbury Plain. Situated on private farmland, no burial has been found within this giant mound which may be an earthen effigy of the planet Jupiter.

Located around 7 miles (11 kilometres) south lies Stonehenge which corresponds with Saturn. Stonehenge's outer linteled stone circle once contained 30 standing stones. Saturn takes 30 years to complete one round of the zodiacal belt which may have dictated the number of standing stones. Astrologically, Saturn is Father Time, the Lord of Karma and a bridge between the material consciousness inherent in the ordinary aspects of life and the higher consciousness of the outermost planets. Stonehenge is a portal between worlds, a megalithic gateway that, once passed through, shifts perception from the personal into the transpersonal and universal realms. For some, Stonehenge confronts you with a reflection of what is hidden within, what must be exposed and transcended. For others, the gateway leads to the inner realms in preparation for an archetypal level of awareness. Stonehenge puts you in touch with yourself and the Cosmos.

Certainly, this planetary ley system connects the most important, and largest, sacred sites in England to one another and symbolically depicts Heaven on Earth. Although, it must be noted that none of the planets is actually orbiting Earth, and their orbits are not circular. As we reach the outer planets these anomalies increase. For example, Pluto has a mean distance from the sun of 3,666.874 million miles (5901 million kilometres) or 39.53 Astronomical Units AU (the distance between the sun and Earth is 1 AU or 93 million miles (149 million kilometres), although this may vary due to its elliptical orbit. Furthermore, a planet's distance from Earth will differ depending on which side of the sun it lies. However, using the same mathematical system that the ancients applied, which uses the mean distance of the planet from Earth in a projected circular orbit, Laurence Upton and I extended the ley and calculated the positions of the outer Saturnian planets of Uranus, Neptune and Pluto, which were not yet discovered in Duke's era. Uranus was discovered in 1781, Neptune in 1846 and Pluto, the outermost member of the solar system, in 1930. Duke's planetarium is not accurately drawn to scale, so any system built around it has an in-built imprecision, or flexibility, but an approximation calculated from the distances from Silbury to his Jupiter and Saturn sites suggests a workable scale which we could use. The distances from Silbury would be approximately Uranus 35 miles (56 kilometres), Neptune 55 miles (88 kilometres) and Pluto 72 miles (115 kilometres).

Our main interest was to see if these planets would correspond to a sacred site. If so, it would suggest that the outer Saturnian planets, unknown to Duke's generation, were known to our remote ancestors. Laurence and I are both astrologers and we began to appreciate the precision involved in the laying out of this ley and its sacred sites. Anchoring an astronomical framework, the ley was aligned to 275 degrees (5 degrees Capricorn), where 0 degrees is West (0 degrees Aries).

Nodal points and the extended ley

Analysing Edward Duke's original diagram, we realised that the orbits of the planets have two 'nodal points' of reference. These are the points where the planetary orbits cross the ley north and south. Duke placed planets with male associations to the south (south node) and those that were traditionally female were shown at the north node. Duke only used one nodal point of reference and we suspected the ley-astronomers used both. Our suspicions proved correct as a large long barrow, the largest of its kind in the Avebury area, was once sited upon Mercury's northern node. Sadly, the site was destroyed in 1967; however, one remaining stone can be found at St Mary's church, Winterbourne Monkton, covering the grave of the Reverend Brinsden who died in 1710. The south node of Venus, incidentally, would pass close to the Barge Inn, by the Kennet and Avon canal at Honey Street!

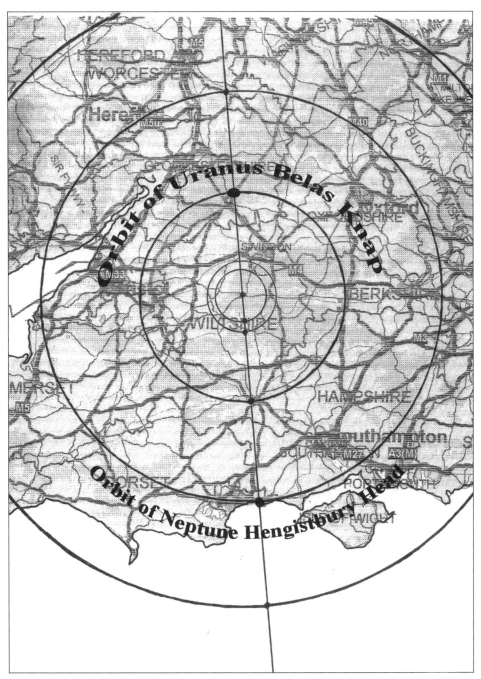

The extended Duke Line
Calculated in 1999 by Laurence Upton and Maria Wheatley

The outer Saturnian planets

Belas Knap - Uranus

Uranus was discovered in the early 18th century by the astronomer William Herschel, yet 6,000 years ago its relative position in the heavens was laid out in the landscape. We found the north node of Uranus at Belas Knap, a fine Neolithic long barrow near Charlton, on the ancient Cotswold Way. Its south node is near the River Avon in the region of Aldershot in Hampshire. Uranus is the light of illumination. The first seven planets represent the forces of life which affect each person individually as well as the humankind collectively. The three outer planets symbolize vibrations of cosmic energy. Uranus energy can stimulate the intuitive facilities, inventive power and connects us to one another as a whole creating true brotherhood/sisterhood.

Following the Duke line north from Belas Knap towards Redditch, the line runs for awhile alongside the Ryknild Way, a Roman Road that lies at 280 degrees (10 degrees Capricorn). Neptune's north node lies near Alcester, which is also on the Ryknild Way. Pluto's north node is found to reside in the inner depths of Birmingham, around the urbanized Edgbaston area. How far the line extends northwards is not yet known, but it is interesting to note that, if followed to its logical conclusion, it takes us close to John O'Groats, the most northerly point of Britain. Heading south, the line extends to Hengistbury Head, on the Wiltshire/Hampshire Avon in Christchurch Bay, near Bournemouth, and this watery spot is where the south node of Neptune's underwater domain is to be found. Close to this coastline we can bathe in Neptunian energy. Neptune is the higher octave of Venus and the Winterbourne Basset stone circle. Despite being millions of miles away from Earth, and thus totally invisible to the naked eye, Neptune was personified by our ancestors as the Gods Poseidon and Neptune.

Neptune is a great Teacher which opens our hearts to Mankind's highest expression, unconditional love. Neptune is associated with the emotions and realms of psychic activity. However, its watery nature requires the cleansing of the emotional body, to clear the astral body of all impurities, so that true psychic visions and mystical inspirations can manifest. However, like a clever magician, Neptune can deceive, create delusion and like the mists that rise from the water obscure the lay of the land and lead us down a wayward path. Hence, Neptune can be the dreamer, drug addict, or in contrast the saint or poet. Cutting through the delusion promises clarity and can bring us into contact with Master Souls and Cosmic Truths.

Pluto's northern node is located in Edgbaston. Close to this point, an emergency archaeology excavation unearthed the remains of a Neolithic long barrow; a suitable counterpart as Pluto is Lord of the Underworld. Pluto is the last member of the sun's family and serves the solar system as eliminator and renewer. In his eliminator guise Pluto has always been associated with death and the afterlife. Pluto can also regenerate and bring deep esoteric wisdom that leads to a breakthrough in consciousness. A Greek custom was to place the ripe seeds of the harvest in large jars and place them in chambers that acted as a refrigerator. The following spring the seeds would be sown and a new harvest would be reaped. Likewise, Pluto's energy within long barrows creates a geophysical arena, which has physical and metaphysical properties symbolizing the renewal of the life force, transmutation of energy and the circle of life that had no beginning and no end.

The planetary circles

Investigating the planetary circles made the system even more credible. Each circle has a dowseable energy field associated with ancient sites and settlements. For instance, the diameter of the sun's orbit at Avebury is one and a half miles (2.41 kilometres), which is the exact length of Avebury's megalithic avenues, and may have symbolized the sun's movement through the signs of the zodiac.

Avebury Henge and Draco the celestial dragon

Writing in 1912, Harold Bayley made additional celestial observations. He noted that the small village of Draycot, which lies to the north of Avebury, and a hill close to Syrencot, north of Stonehenge, represents Draco the dragon, a circumpolar constellation. Currently, at the summer solstice, the bright star Eltanin, 'the head of Draco', is in vertical alignment to both Avebury and Stonehenge. In 3500 BC, Eltanin's rising was visible through the central passages of the temples of Hathor at Denderah and of Mut at Thebes. According to Sir Norman Lockyer Eltanin became the orientation point of the great Carnac Temples of Rameses and Khons at Thebes.

The European ley system

Other remarkable ley systems were created which were used to determine cycles of time. One outstanding example was discovered by Xavier Guichard near Geneva, on the French-Swiss border. At the turn of the last century Guichard began to research the origins of European place-names in his native home of France. After 25 years of study he concluded that three primary names existed: Antium, Burgus and Alesia. In ancient Greece Alesia was Eleusis and in the Indo-European culture Alles meant 'a meeting place to which people travelled'. He noted the place-names, and he found over 400 in France alone, were often associated with similar landscape features, such as hills overlooking rivers, springs, or salt deposits. He concluded that the primary place-names were once ceremonial meeting places which were intimately associated with water – springs, rivers or lakes.

Further investigations revealed an extraordinary ley network incorporating mathematical and astronomical precision consisting of twenty-four lines radiating from a central location – 'Alaise' – which targeted similar place-names with similar topographical features. The lines divide the horizon into equal segments that mark the meridian, equinoxes and solstices. Guichard proposed that a mathematical unit was applied to calculate the system as there is a mean distance of 15 degrees between each line.

The astrological great year

My research shows that encoded into the ley system is an astrological 'clock' which can be used to determine cycles of time, from a 24-hour day to an astrological Great Year. It takes approximately 25,920 years for the precession of the equinoxes to make one complete passage within the belt of the constellations of the zodiac – an astrological Great Year. Intriguingly, if each ley represents 1080 years the entire system of 24 leys (1080 x 24) equates precisely to 25,920 years - an astrological Great Year. Prehistoric mathematicians set the numerical value of 1080 and the Great Year into the vast Alaise ley system dedicating it to the Divine Feminine.

Sacred number – the Divine Feminine

According to the late John Michell 1080 is a sacred number. 1,080 miles (1739 kilometres) is the radius of the moon, the sacred Greek phase τό γαίου Лυεύμα numerically adds up to 1,080 meaning the *spirit of the Earth*, and 1,080 is the number of breaths traditionally drawn in one hour. Furthermore, throughout the ancient world 1,080 was a divine number representing the receptive, yin

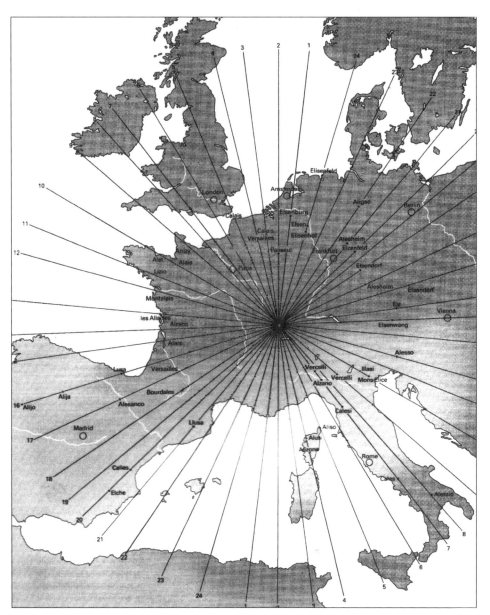

The ley network

side of nature, associated with the mystical moon, its influence on the waters within the earth, prophecy and intuition. Michell points out that Stonehenge encoded this canonical number within the inner and outer sarsen rings, and it was used to determine the dimensions of Teotihuacan. The opposite of 1,080 is 666, the number of the beast, which Michell says signifies the positive or active charge of solar energy, associated with the tyrant or emperor. Evidently, our ancient ancestors not only sited sacred sites upon leys but also created complex mathematical and astronomical ley systems. Interestingly, CERN the particle accelerator that lies on the Franco-Swiss border close to Geneva is aligned on the ley network. World leaders invariably meet in Geneva when important discussions and decisions are to be made.

A similar ley system of 24 lines was laid out in the grounds of Badminton House, Gloucestershire, which is the principal seat of the Dukes of Beaufort since the late 17th century.

Ley grids

Guy Ragland Phillips explores leys in his book *Brigantia – A Mysteriography*. Guy discovered the longest ley in Britain; the Belinus ley which was associated with a ley system. Each north-south and east-west line was separated by 12 miles (19.31 kilometres). The system seemed to pivot on the Belinus ley which has been thoroughly researched by Gary Biltcliffe and Caroline Hoare and will be discussed later.

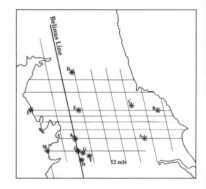

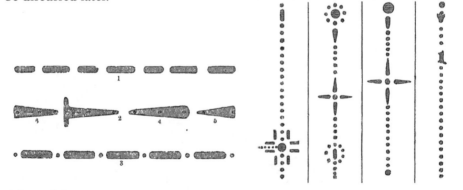

Mound Leys

Native American peoples marked the course of leys by constructing mounds and earthworks upon them. Dead straight mound lines coursed for miles across the land. One antiquarian recorded for prosperity: *I observed a lineal range of mounds running north west, which I afterward traced to the Spring Grove, a distance of about one hundred miles [160 kilometres], running west from an altar near the tail of a [serpent mound] effigy. Sadly, many of the mound-leys that adorned the Iowa countryside near Turkey River were destroyed making way for a railway.*

Locating a ley

Locating leys is a relatively simple task. Using a large scale OS map look for old medieval churches, cathedrals, priories, manor houses and monasteries; prehistoric man made mounds, standing stones, brochs, hill forts, stone circles, medicine wheels, ancient Native American centres such as Newark, or those which have been urbanized such as Circleville, holy wells or any other site of antiquity. Five or more sites which align in a linear fashion indicate a local ley. Lines that contain seven sites often indicate a chakra ley with each site representing a particular chakra and I call twelve sites in linear alignment a 'zodiac ley'. Many of the great USA centres, such as Chillicothe and Newark, form powerful ley alignments and complex ley systems.

Interacting and dowsing leys

Once you have located a ley you can dowse and interact with its energy.

- Position yourself in close proximity to where the ley flows.

- Visualize the target as a linear line of silver light and ask the dowsing rod to 'show you the direction of the ley'. The rod will waver and eventually it will point to the direction of the ley.

- Align yourself with that direction and slowly walk forward with the rod in 'search' mode until it swings to the 'found' position. This is one edge of the ley, which is known as the 'leading edge'.

- Return the rod to 'search' and continue the dowsing pass. When the rod swings into 'found' the trailing edge has been located, denoting the width of the ley.

- Some leys have a central energy band running between the leading and trailing edges, which is especially strong. Using a quartz crystal the line's energy can be manipulated to cut off or reduce the ley's energy flow. My father studied this central line and showed that it could be used alongside dowsing in a binary operation of 'on's' and 'off's' through which Morse code type messages could be transmitted across vast distances. In the 1990s at Swindon College, Wiltshire, using several students, a wooden screen and energetically charged stones he publicly demonstrated how charged stones and leys could be used for simple communication purposes.

*Callanish is one of the most magnificent
stone circles that I have dowsed.*

*Energies rise out of the ground
bathing you in Gaia's energy.*

CHAPTER 3
Dragon currents and genesis leys

Long distance leys have yin and yang earth energy currents entwining them. In the 1980s, Hamish Miller and Paul Broadhurst, authors of *The Sun and the Serpent*, discovered that two earth energy currents coil around the St Michael ley in a caduceus-like fashion. Prehistoric sites were aligned upon the currents dating to the Early Neolithic (4000 BC). They called the currents *Mary and Michael* as numerous churches dedicated to St Michael were located on the Michael current and churches dedicated to the Virgin Mary or Mary Magdalene were positioned on the female current. Evidently the Knights Templar and medieval Masons were acutely aware of the twin currents and positioned their holy sites upon them.

Authors Gary Biltcliffe and Caroline Hoare discovered that Britain's longest ley, the Belinus ley, is likewise associated with yin and yang energy currents. The twin dragon currents, Elen and Belinus, are especially powerful and their energies can be experienced at numerous ancient sites which are featured in Gary and Caroline's highly recommended book *The Spine of Albion*.

In 2220 BC yin and yang energy flows were documented by the ancient Chinese. Wherever the dragon lines crossed was revered as sacred space and reserved for the Emperors' tomb, palace or temple. Personifying a place that emits balanced and benign forces, which are conducive to good health, wealth and longevity, the Chinese Feng Shui Masters mapped the entire Chinese landscape and located the dragon line's mystical pathways and sacred crossroads.

Mystical pathways of Rollright

The Rollright Ring in Oxfordshire is a fascinating stone circle where you can experience the Elen and Belinus currents. The Rollright Ring is a Late Neolithic stone circle of oolitic limestone which is a perfect circle of around 72 stones, although legend says the stones cannot be counted! Originally there may have been around 100 stones, standing shoulder to shoulder, creating an almost wall-like effect. In the field on the opposite side of the road stands the outlying, hunchbacked King Stone. Its distorted shape is due to centuries of superstition. Stone chips were taken from the stone for 'good luck' and this accounts for its twisted hunched shape. About a quarter of a mile to the east in the adjacent field stands 'The Whispering Knights', a dolmen (burial chamber) comprising four vertical megaliths and a fallen capstone.

Strange experiences are common within the stone circle and I will never forget a summer performance of Shakespeare's *The Tempest* within the ring as there were constant disruptions. Mobile phones failed, watches inexplicably stopped, a stopwatch lost ten minutes and the professional actors forgot their lines. One dancer saw mysterious strange lights as a vengeful gale and sweeping rain began to lash across the stone circle. A wild night! Rollright is one of my favourite stone circles as it is full of atmosphere and I enjoy taking dowsing groups there. But I always say to people, 'expect the unexpected at the Rollrights!'

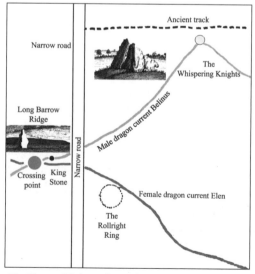

The Elen and Belinus dragon lines at Rollright. Reproduced with kind permission from Gary Biltcliffe adapted from his book 'The Spine of Albion'.

34

Interacting and dowsing the Belinus dragon current

Interestingly, both currents deliberately avoid the Rollright Ring and the female current, Elen, flows by it. Dowse for the male current, Belinus, at the King Stone and the Whispering Knights dolmen.

- With a single rod, or a pair of dowsing rods, in 'search' (pointing straight ahead and parallel to the ground) visualize the earth current in the Earth beneath the monument.

- Silently command the rod/s to *show you the Belinus earth current*. If you can, visualize the target as a meandering river of energy.

- Make a 360° dowsing pass around the monument. When the 'leading' edge of the earth current has been detected the rod/s will swing into the 'found' position.

- Reset the rod/s into 'search' mode and continue the dowsing pass until the rod/s once again swing into the 'found' position. You have successfully located the 'trailing' edge of the current and can estimate its width.

- Dowse for the female earth current, Elen, which courses near the southeast perimeter of the stone circle.

Dragon lines can amplify your thoughts and emotions. It takes a very balanced person to constantly live above dragon energy. Ideally, like our ancestors we should have dragon energy in medicinal doses! Each person's tolerance is different and some people may instantly feel the energy and only need a small dose, whereas others may spend several hours interacting with the energy.

Genesis leys

We have seen that Dragon lines are male/solar and female/lunar serpentine currents and where they cross is considered especially  auspicious. In contrast, a Genesis ley is a hermaphrodite line where male and female energies flow harmoniously together as one imbuing the area with balancing and harmonic energy.

My late father discovered that Genesis energy lines emerge from one location and flow across the landscape for a short distance, or sometimes several miles, before descending into the ground and terminating. They can meander like a river or be relatively straight and their characteristic feature is that they emerge from the ground and form two-ram horn spirals which are highly energizing.

One is clockwise, the other counter-clockwise; they are male and female vortices forming a distinctive serpent tail. One sacred site may be associated with the emerging energy, another with the descending energy and several sacred sites may be positioned along the hermaphrodite line.

Locating Genesis lines

In the Avebury landscape Brain Ashley discovered the 'Beckhampton Serpent', a powerful Genesis line which emerges from several ram-horns on Knoll Down. It flows into Avebury's southern inner circle bringing harmonic and balancing energies to the site. Another exceptionally powerful Genesis line emerges from two ram-horn spirals on Dragon Hill, near the White Horse of Uffington, Oxfordshire. Gaining strength and power as it courses through the ground the hermaphrodite line flows above the White Horse and then courses along the raised rampart of Uffington Castle, a Druidic magico-ceremonial centre. The line then flows along the axis of Wayland's Smithy long barrow; here it pulsates at seven points creating a chakra-like axis line. Finally, it descends deep into the Earth at the central chamber. I suspect this section of the line was used to balance and cleanse the chakra system before entering the chamber which may have been used for oracle visions and initiation ceremonies. Many people experience a sense of peace and harmony, are able to commune with the Earth, or discover or sense their spiritual purpose within the chamber's protective confines.

Wayland's Smithy and the Genesis line

Genesis lines are exceptionally powerful and their serpentine flow creates an unseen sub-terrestrial river. They become highly energized at the full moon and solar flares and sunspot activity enhances their power which the monuments absorb.

Native American geomancers identified the Genesis current and often marked its course with earthen mounds in the shape of a serpent. Close to the Mississippi River, at the junction of the Turkey River, a mound land-serpent once snaked across the land for over 2 and a half miles (4 kilometres).

Interacting and dowsing a genesis line

Locate the spiral ram-horns and emerging energy upon Dragon hill and follow the energy current across the landscape.

Remote dowsing

Over the years I have developed a dowsing system which I call *remote dowsing*. It is a valuable tool when extracting information about long lost sites and ancient civilizations. Have a go at dowsing the serpent mound illustrations with a pendulum. Divine where the energy emerges and descends on each of the land serpents. Now tune into the landscape. What do you see, hear or smell? Use the five senses to experience the environ and the sixth sense to divine it.

Although I cannot say with certainty there is no reason why an extended Genesis ley should not be a great global line encircling the Earth. Symbolically it would look like the alchemic symbol of wholeness, the ouroboros. The energy may repeatedly emerge and descend as it courses along creating powerful nodal points which may have been marked by power places.

Earth chimneys are often associated with
Iron Age hill forts and Druid ceremonial centres,
such as Figsbury Ring, Wiltshire.

CHAPTER 4
Earth chimneys

European dowsers have noted a worldwide energy phenomenon that connects the Earth to the Cosmos. Guy Tisson, a French diviner, noted an exotic geometry manifests approximately every 32 feet (10 metres) across the landmass of the Earth. Its geo-signature is easy to identify as it consists of seven concentric circles of energy, the largest of which is usually around 19 feet (6 metres) in circumference and between 1-9 looped arms or petals extending from the centre and spread some 19-29 feet (6-9 metres) outwards.

There are two types of chimneys; some are going 'upwards' connecting the Earth to the cosmos whilst others are going 'downwards' from the cosmos to Earth. Chimneys are the essential breathing points upon the Earth which have a regular breathing rhythm; an inhaling phase, followed by a pause, and then they exhale.

Certain chimneys are nurturing to all forms of life and can be excellent places to meditate as they act as a spiritual gateway connecting you to the Earth and the cosmos simultaneously allowing you to experience direct Oneness with life. Meditating above this geo-glyph can be a profound and emotional encounter – a truly sacred experience. They can be seen as active portals and gateways to contact celestial beings. However, some chimneys can drain you of energy and so it is vitally important to establish their energetic quality.

Interacting and dowsing an earth chimney

Chimneys interlace the planet manifesting every 32 feet (10 metres), so they can be dowsed anywhere. At large European cathedrals chimneys can be found at the altar.

- With a single rod, or a pair of dowsing rods, in 'search' (pointing straight ahead and parallel to the ground) visualize the earth chimney in the ground.
- Silently command the rod/s to 'show you the nearest earth chimney'.
- Follow the rod until it swings into the 'found' position. The rod normally takes you to the centre of the geometry.
- Visualize the concentric circles of energy and slowly walk forwards. You will get seven 'found' reactions as you walk away from the centre. You can tune into one of the circles and follow it.

Experience the breathing phases

Earth's breathing points can be experienced as they have a regular breathing rhythm - an inhaling phase followed by a pause and then they exhale.

- Place a rod or pendulum over the centre of the chimney and it will swing either clockwise (representing an inhaling phase) or counter-clockwise (representing an exhaling phase).
- After a while the rod or pendulum will lose its momentum and pause.
- Eventually it will begin to swing, building up its momentum in the opposite direction.
- Get a friend to stand close to you and both repeat the dowsing exercise and you will notice the pendulum swings are in unison.
- Experience the inhaling and exhaling phases and note how they make you feel.

  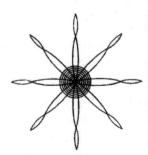

Dowsing the arms

Use information dowsing to establish how many arms the chimney manifests. Now make a 360-degree dowsing pass around the outside of the concentric circles whilst tuning into the arms. When an arm has been located the rod/s will swing into the 'found' position. Reset the rod/s into 'search' mode and repeat the procedure until all of the arms have been located.

Now proceed to the next chimney, which is located 32 feet (10 metres) away and repeat the above exercise. If the inhaling and exhaling phases are identical to the first chimney, which is determined by counting the number of gyrations in each cycle, the chimneys are said to be 'twinned'.

As above and so below

As above and so below is an old occult adage. This timeless lore suggests that whatever the Earth manifests the heavens should also. We can therefore imagine celestial leys coursing across space, ley systems that connect planets within a solar system and larger galactic energy points creating cosmic energy centres in deep space.

*Geodetic aquastat lines tend to be associated
with mounds or raised earthworks.*

*Silbury Hill close to Avebury Henge is sited
upon a large geospiral and numerous aquastat lines
converge and emerge from this regional power centre.*

CHAPTER 5
The geodetic system of earth energies

In the late 1980s, John Martineau, the founder of *Wooden Books*, saved the manuscripts and surveys of the late Guy Underwood from a fire. Without his intervention an entire life's work of researching archaeological sites and Earth energies would have been lost. John kindly gave the collection to my late father who became a world authority on dowsing the *geodetic system of earth energies* and I am continuing his work.

Guy was a field archaeologist, and one of the world's greatest Master Dowsers. During the 1940s-1960s, he worked alongside renowned archaeologists such as Cyril Fox and J. F. Stone. After several archaeological excavations he became acutely aware that the planet's surface was interlaced with a distinctive earth energy system, which he called the *geodetic system of earth energies*. This was a seminal discovery but more revelations followed when he discovered that megalithic monuments such as Stonehenge had their foundation plans carefully integrated to conform to the geodetic system's flows and courses. Earlier we saw the spectacular geodetic geometries that Guy re-discovered, such as the geospiral and halo patterns, and now we will look at the geodetic lines.

Divining the land

Guy found numerous long-lost prehistoric sites in the southwest of England and he did so by 'reading the land', detecting the geodetic energy lines and spiral patterns. Today dowsers employ *information dowsing* and use the '*show me*' technique to find lost sites, or to locate underground water. In contrast, Guy adopted the same divining techniques as the ancients; he followed the geodetic energy lines, which led him to the esoteric centre of the site. He was very successful and was the first archaeologist and dowser to discover a Bronze Age road, long-lost stone circles, hill figures and Roman temples. Using dowsing he found an exquisite – and rare – Bronze Age gold artefact known as the

'Sun Disk', which is on display in the British Museum. Guy realized that the Earth produces extraordinary energy lines which emit a strong and numerical force. My own research has furthered his understanding of the geodetic system which reveals how the Earth can promote healing.

The geodetic system of earth energies

Geodetic lines are especially powerful as they generate a force field which can extend as far as 90 feet (27.43 metres). There are three distinctive geodetic energy flows which are called the *water line, track line* and *aquastat line*. Guy never fully explained their significance and, for the first time, their remarkable qualities are revealed.

Underground yang water – three lines of force

In *The Essential Dowsing Guide* an underground stream was briefly described as a *water line triad* which is often called a *stream band*. The stream band is the surface pattern of an underground stream flowing predominantly with yang water. It manifests three energy lines and either side of it are *secondary parallels*, which are a mirror image of the main stream band as shown in the illustration.

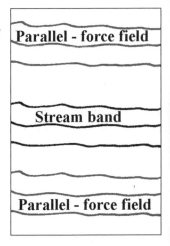

Geomancers and dowsers agree that underground water is injurious to health; living above yang water for prolonged periods can weaken the immune system and promote dis-ease.

The Parallels

Parallels are energy lines that run parallel to the main stream. Professional dowsers have noted that if a parallel is followed it will lead you on a circular course, bringing you back to where you started, as shown in the following illustration. These circular energy fields are in constant motion expanding and contracting and they generate a detectable energy field.

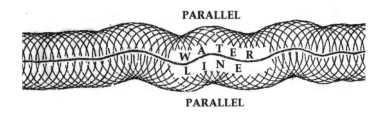

PARALLEL

PARALLEL

Interacting and dowsing water lines

The Show Me method

- Use information dowsing to determine if the location is associated with an underground stream.

- If the answer is 'yes' ask the dowsing rod to 'show you the direction of the nearest underground stream' and spend a moment visualizing an underground stream in the vicinity. The rod will waver and eventually point to the direction of the underground stream. Align yourself with that direction and slowly walk forward until the rod/s swing into the 'found' position. This is one of the triad water lines.

- Return the rod/s to 'search' and very slowly move forward. When the rod/s swing into the 'found' position the second water line has been located. Repeat the procedure until you have located the third. Over a small underground stream the triad lines are usually very close together. Guy called these 'hairlines' which have no appreciable width and they are easily missed by the beginner in which case only one line is found.

- Larger streams generate three sets of triads (nine hairlines).

- Although rare, exceptionally large underground rivers generate nine triads (27 hairlines).

Dowse the parallels

- Tune into the parallel lines by visualizing them. Now use the 'show me' command and slowly walk away from the main triad. The rod/s will swing into the 'found' position upon detecting one of the parallels. You will notice that they are 'weaker' than the main triad.

- Repeat the exercise to find the other two parallels. The distance from the centre of the stream band to the first parallel is equal to the underground depth of the stream. This is known as the Bishop's depthing method, which is a rough calculation.

- Now tune into one of the parallel lines and follow it and you will be led on a circular course which will bring you back to where you started.

- Determine if there are any more underground streams in the vicinity and dowse for them in a similar manner.

The geodetic dowsing method

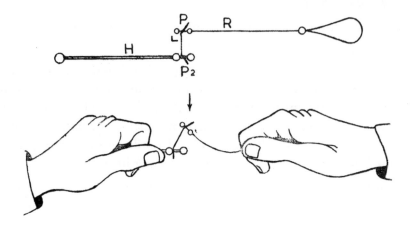

Unlike other earth energies, geodetic lines affect different sides of the physical body. Geodetic energies which affect the left side of the body are considered *negative* and those affecting the right side of the body are *positive*. Guy invented a small dowsing rod and developed a new dowsing technique that utilizes the body's sensitivity to geodetic energies. However, the geodetic rod can be difficult to use and take time to master. My dowsing students often employ geodetic dowsing techniques whilst using a metal L-rod. Geodetic dowsing does not use the 'show me' technique and you do not need to attune or visualize the target. You simply hold a dowsing rod in a particular manner. When it detects a geodetic line that is influencing the body it will swing into the 'found' position. This method creates a sensitive link between you and the geodetic energy that you are divining. (See Appendix 2. *The Geodetic Rod* for more details.)

Regardless of which dowsing method you choose, finding geodetic lines is a essential as you will be able to identify geopathic stress zones (inharmonious energies) and, as we shall soon see, harmonic energy that is beneficial to all life forms. Experiment with both dowsing methods and choose which one suits you best.

Geodetic dowsing - locating an underground yang stream

- Hold a single dowsing rod *strongly* in the left hand; this is because a water line is considered negative which affects the left hand side of the body.

- Make sure the handgrip strength remains consistent during the dowsing pass and each time you dowse for an underground triad water line. This is 'rod-body programming.'

- Walk anywhere you choose maintaining the grip. Begin by walking around a room in your home, or divine your garden for underground streams.

- Upon detecting a triad line the rod will swing into the 'found' position.

- Return the rod to 'search' and slowly move a pace or so forward. When the rod swings into 'found' position the second line has been located. Repeat the procedure until you have located the third line. Over a small underground stream the triad lines are usually very close together. Underwood called these 'hairlines' which have no appreciable width and they are easily missed by the beginner in which case only one line is found. As mentioned earlier larger streams generate three sets of triads (nine hairlines) and exceptionally large underground rivers generate nine triads (27 hairlines).

Dowse for the parallels

- Continue to walk away from the triad line but hold the rod with a slightly lighter grip and dowse for the parallels.

- The rod will swing into the 'found' position upon detecting one of the parallels.

- Repeat the exercise to find the other parallels.

- Now tune into one of the parallel lines and follow it and you will be led on a circular course which will bring you back to where you started.

Crossing streams and chronic geopathic stress

Underground streams that cross at a near right-angle produce severe geopathic stress. Long-term exposure is especially injurious to health and short-term exposure can produce feelings of apathy and depression. Underwood noted the crossing streams produce a distinctive pattern which he called a 'reversed circle'. A spiral necklace forms in each quadrant which face outwards unlike the positive healing necklaces of the geospiral which face inward.

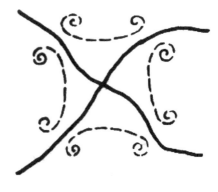

To our ancestors the outward facing spiral implied a lack of spiritual protection. Places of execution, such as the gallows at Tower Hill, London, and blind houses (circular or rectangular buildings with only small slits for windows that were used as temporary prisons for condemned persons) were all deliberately sited upon this toxic pattern. The esoteric meaning was that the inmate was a 'deodand' – or 'one given to God'. The spiral necklaces turn away from the victim denoting a lack of divine protection and produce a delayed effect on the nervous system, such as feelings of foreboding, dejection and gloom. Hauntings, poltergeists and malefic spirits are attracted to the pattern and in my experience gain strength from it. Is this where the symbol of the 'X' meaning 'wrong answer' (unprotected location) originated from?

A track line – six lines of force

In open countryside animals instinctively sense, and follow, geodetic track lines. Many of England's old country lanes and roads were first trodden out by animals following them and this accounts for their meandering and twisting course. Track lines emit harmonic energy which is thought to relax the muscles whilst gently stimulating physical energy levels, and this is why migrating animals follow them and ancient man sited roads and tracks upon them. The alignment has an additional advantage in that animals driven along such tracks follow them naturally and are less likely to stray. This is why all old droves, which are ancient Iron Age roads used for driving cattle along, are always aligned upon them.

The track line consists of two parallel triads with an interval between them. Track lines are positive and beneficial to most life forms. They produce between 2-5 sets of *secondary parallels* similar to the water triad line, but with the important distinction that they are not circular in form and can be followed

1st parallel - force field

8 - 15 ft

8 - 15 ft

1st parallel - force field

as separate lines. The parallels are found between 8-15 feet (2.43-4.57 metres) from the primary track line and repeat at diminishing distances until they become indistinguishable at 40-70 feet (12.19-21.33 metres). Geoff Jenkins, who often dowsed alongside Guy and taught me how to use the geodetic rod, noted that hedge-mounds or hedges are frequently aligned on the parallels.

Geodetic lines are easy to identify as each flow contains a specific number of energy lines making pattern recognition simple. They are exceptionally powerful as they generate parallels creating an extensive force field.

Interacting and dowsing track lines

The Show Me method

- Dowse old country roads and lanes, ancient trails and Neolithic roads such as ridgeways or Iron Age droves; also animal trails across open countryside.

- Follow the procedure for dowsing the water line, but tune into a track line and visualize its pattern of six lines.

- Dowse the parallels. Notice that they can be followed as independent lines.

The geodetic dowsing method

Practise dowsing old country roads or choose a field which has a noticeable animal trail.

- Hold a dowsing rod *strongly* in the right hand; this is because a track line is considered positive which affects the right-hand side of the body.

- Make sure the handgrip strength remains consistent during the dowsing pass and each time you dowse a track line. This is 'rod-body programming'.

- Walk across an old lane or track. The dowsing rod will react to each track line.

- Continue walking and maintaining the 'grip' and at approximately 8-15 feet (2.43-4.57 metres), the first secondary parallel will be detected. Now walk another 8-15 feet (2.43-4.57 metres) and you will locate yet another parallel, which is weaker than the first and so on.

An Aquastat line – twelve lines of healing force

In the 1940s, Guy Underwood discovered an energy line which consists of twelve very thin hairlines which he called an 'aquastat'. He never explained what an aquastat was other than some sort of energy line associated with water, hence the term aquastat. I spent many hours reading through his notes on aquastats and found no clarification. Over the years, many people have asked me, *what is an aquastat line? And what is the difference between a water line and an aquastat line?* Guy himself seemed very confused and puzzled over the problem. About five years ago I discovered the answer. An aquastat is an underground stream that flows predominantly with yin water. It emits a harmonic

49

energy field which boosts the immune system and promotes longevity. As we will see later, this harmonic field can be measured for its hertz frequency which provides evidence for its therapeutic properties.

Aquastats consist of two pairs of triad lines with a gap between them and they produce 2-5 sets of *secondary parallels* similar to track lines. The parallels are found at 15 and 30 feet (4.57-9.14 metres) from the outer aquastat line and, like the primary aquastat line, they release harmonic energy. A single aquastat line and its parallels can produce a healing energy field which is over 100 feet wide! Later, we will see how this energy responds to our thoughts.

Healing energy

Living above aquastat energy is especially beneficial and one extraordinary example shows that it produced mass healing. The Chislehurst Caves in Kent contain over twenty miles (32 kilometres) of underground galleries which are thought to be of prehistoric origin. They were used extensively during World War II as air raid shelters and over 15,000 people took refuge in them, many of whom lived underground permanently as their homes were destroyed. During 1959-60, it was widely reported by the media that many elderly people who stayed in the caves were miraculously cured of rheumatism. We discovered that the caves and many other manmade galleries are aligned upon aquastats creating healing environments. Our research shows that some aquastats can be dry. Remarkably, long after the yin water has gone a healing force continues to be emitted, although the energy field is much weaker than its water-filled counterpart.

Interacting and dowsing aquastat lines

The Show Me method

Dowse sacred sites, mounds, raised earthworks, and open countryside for aquastats.

- Follow the procedure for dowsing the track line, but tune into an aquastat line which manifests 12 lines as shown in the illustration. When divining aquastats which are the most important geodetic lines in the design layout of an ancient site. You will get six dowsing reactions, followed by a gap then another six reactions. These divine veins of Gaia reveal the healing zones within temple space.

- Use information dowsing to check if the aquastat is wet or dry.

- A beginner may not discern all of the individual triad lines in which case only four reactions are obtained for each set of triads.

- Locate the parallels.

The geodetic dowsing method

- Hold a rod in the right hand; this is because an aquastat line is positive and affects the right-hand side of the body. However, the grip must be lighter than the track line grip so that the rod responds to aquastat energy only.

- Make sure the handgrip remains consistent during the dowsing pass and each time you dowse an aquastat line. This is 'rod-body programming'.

- Walk anywhere you choose maintaining the same consistent grip. Practise at a sacred site or in the open countryside.

- Upon detecting an aquastat line the rod will swing into the 'found' position.

- Aquastats consist of two pairs of triads running parallel so dowse for all twelve lines. A gap separates the two pairs.

- The beginner may not discern all of the individual triad lines, in which case only four reactions are obtained for each set of triads.

- Continue walking and at approximately 15-30 feet (4.57-9.14 metres), you will detect the first secondary parallel. Walk another 15-30 feet (4.57-9.14 metres) and you will locate another parallel, which is weaker than the first parallel and so on.

- Use information dowsing to check if the aquastat is wet or dry.

Harmonic crossing points

I discovered that when two aquastat lines cross at a near right-angle they create a harmonic pattern which emits harmonic energy. The pattern is opposite to the reversed circle that Underwood discovered which emits inharmonious energy. The spirals face inward signifying divine protection. This is an ideal location for a healing room, surgical theatre, or recovery room and so on.

I have found this energy pattern within stone circles and frequently at Celtic hill forts and believe the cross and circle (Celtic Cross) was seen as a protective and healing symbol by the Druids and the Early Christians based on this earth pattern.

Divining Stonehenge for aquastats

The prehistoric architects were fully aware of the mysterious aquastatic force and sited standing stones, earthen mounds and holy complexes upon them to create healing temple spaces and to distribute the energy. The survey below shows the many aquastat lines that are generated by two blind springs/geospirals at Stonehenge which are marked by the Heel Stone and the Altar Stone.

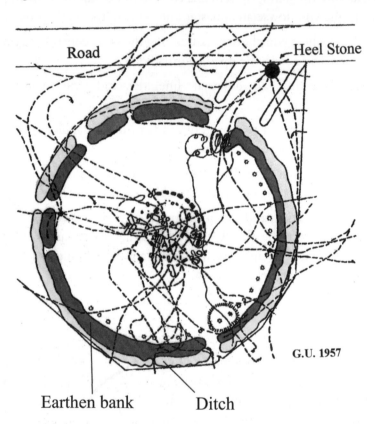

Road   Heel Stone

G.U. 1957

Earthen bank   Ditch

Healing Stones

When a standing stone is rooted into aquastat energy it gives the stone magico-healing properties. Subtly carved features known as cup marks or basins can enhance and direct its flow. The energy is released from the basin in a Fibonacci spiral of pure energy and then it encloses the stone with the Earth's healing life force. Below is Guy Underwood's survey of the Slaughter Stone at Stonehenge which shows several carved basins that mark the locations and diameters of aquastat spiral energy. Guy visited Stonehenge over 200 times and created the most detailed earth energy survey of the site to date.

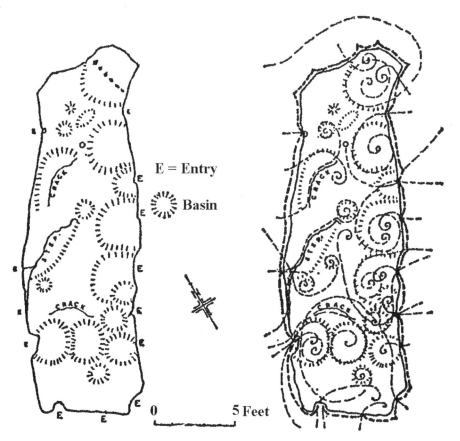

E = Entry

Basin

0   5 Feet

The Slaughter Stone, Stonehenge
Feel the energy with the palm of your hand. Seven chakra basins were carved into the stone

Energy experiment

Ancient geomancers were aware that when an object or construct was sited in close proximity to aquastatic energy, the parallels would be drawn towards it and often encase it. Aquastat parallels can outline mounds, hill figures and sections of a temple or religious construct, surrounding it with a vibrant living force field. Undoubtedly, the prehistoric priesthood manipulated the directional flow of aquastat energy. Many years ago two Chinese Feng Shui Masters showed my late father that when meditation and spiritual intent are applied to the aquastat, its parallels, the emitted force field associated with an aquastat stream, would alter its flow-direction by responding to deep alpha and theta brainwaves. Old-style geomants would use a long stick or staff to tap the ground to 'arouse the dragon energy' and use the tapping staff to direct its flow. Further experiments over the course of ten years showed that geodetic water lines, track lines, aquastats (streams), geospirals and haloes have permanence.

The Minnesota Spider

Throughout ancient America there were numerous animal effigies, such as serpents, tortoises, lions, elks and intriguing mystical creatures. One stunning but sadly lost example is the Minnesota Spider. Located upon elevated ground, and overlooking a beautiful prairie, the vast earthen mound spider covered about one acre. No doubt the effigy was encased by a flowing aquastatic force field which symbolically brought it to 'life'. Underwood detected an aquastat outline at the prehistoric White Horse chalk hill figure at Uffington in Oxfordshire.

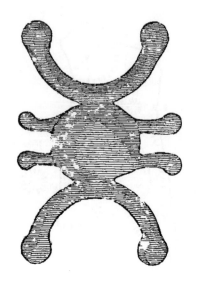

Underwood believed that the geodetic system was generated by the Earth Force, which was always counted in threes (geodetic lines, primary and secondary haloes) and sevens (geospirals), two of numerology's important numbers. In assigning to the planet a form of intelligence in its own right he preceded Professor Lovelock's 'Gaia concept' by some 30 years.

Locating aquastat energy

The Uffington White Horse in Oxfordshire is a chalk hill figure dated to the late Bronze Age. An aquastat flow can be found close to the main outline of the horse, flowing along the head, neck and part of its back.

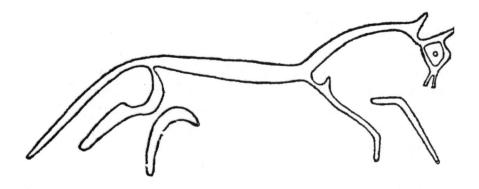

The giant ground figures created by rock alignments and gravel formations representing humans, animals and ritual symbols are found in Baja California, Arizona, California, and Nevada. Around 100 ground figures are in Death Valley, Red Rock Canyon in Kern County, and Wild Rose Canyon in Inyo County and the Chocolate Mountains in Imperial County. Check if the outlines have attracted the distinctive 12-fold aquastat parallel energy.

Holy lines, transformative power

Occasionally a triad water line (yin line) and a magnetic aquastat (yang line) run together and follow a similar course. These are called 'holy lines' and they can be found at important sacred sites of global importance. When they flow co-jointly or at locations where they cross generates exceptionally strong ling energy. Revered by the ancient priesthood and the Masonic Brotherhood, this geodetic combination designated sacred space. An outer section of the old City of London, the Vatican and Stonehenge incorporated holy lines as part of their esoteric design canon. After many years of interacting with holy lines, I discovered that the aquastat energy cleanses and transmutes the nearby water line of its toxic emissions. This reveals that yin water has alchemic, purifying and transformative properties.

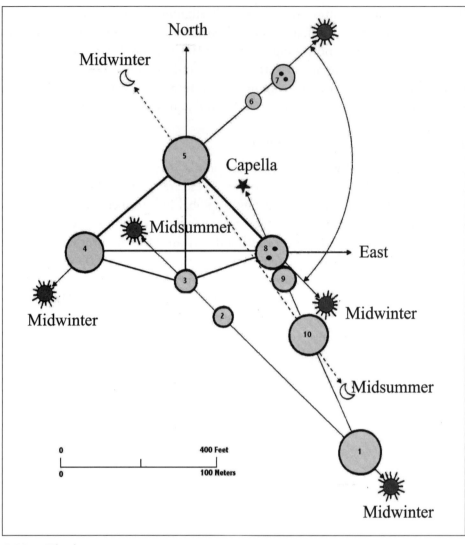

© *Maria Wheatley*

*Powerful reticulating geodetic flows are associated
with Odry stone circles in Poland.*

*During WWII Gestapo leader Heinrich Himmler
gave the order to cordon off the monument,
and it become an occult destination for Nazi 'pilgrimages'.*

CHAPTER 6
Following geodetic lines

In their progression through the Earth's surface geodetic energy lines can flow in an undulating manner, form zigzags, create spirals or folded loops. The way in which they flow reveals information about the underlying geological conditions and the line's relative speed, for instance, when a geodetic line courses across rocky sub-soils it will invariably form a pointed zigzag energy pattern. This was first noted in 1899 by the water diviner Benjamin Tompkins. Flowing across chalk, limestone or clay beds geodetic lines often meander, but if they pass small pockets of water or rock they will form spirals and zigzag flows respectively.

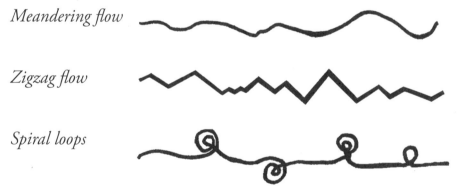

Meandering flow

Zigzag flow

Spiral loops

Folded loops

When a geodetic line begins to slow down it forms folded loops.

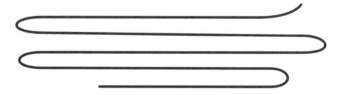

Reticulated lines

At some point in their course the lines will cross one another to form reticulated lines indicating the line is fast flowing and these are shown in the illustration.

'A' shows the flow of a track line, 'B' a water line and 'C' an aquastat flow. The two outer lines of a waterline, the two halves of a track line or aquastat, cross and re-cross each other diagonally.

Life-enhancing energy flows

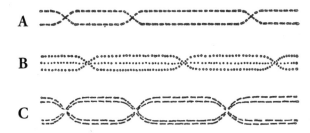

> *Genesis lines and dragon currents, such as Mary and Michael, or Elen and Belinus, meander like mighty rivers across the countryside, whereas geodetic lines can form folded loops, spirals or flow in a zigzag manner.*

One of the most auspicious energy patterns to live above is the branch spiral as it promotes longevity, health and well-being. This aquastatic flow was sought after by our ancestors who sited houses for the living and tombs for the deceased upon it. It is easy to identify as the geodetic line forms spirals which are around 5-20 feet (1.52-6.09 metres) wide.

Interact with branch spirals at long barrows such as the West Kennet long barrow in Wiltshire and Belas Knap in Gloucestershire; also, the stone dolmen chambers, altars, and crypts of Danbury, Connecticut; South Woodstock, Vermont; Mystery Hill, Vermont.

Alchemic spirals – protective power

Geodetic lines and geospirals influence one another and generate harmonic ling energy. When a geodetic line enters the energy field of a geospiral, primary and secondary haloes, it will cause a gap in the pattern to occur. The powerful spirals of the geospiral will also cause the geodetic line to suddenly take a spiral course and this effect is called a *primary spiral*. A geospiral pattern can produce several primary spirals according to the number of geodetic lines which converge there. Spiral energy patterns are beneficial and the primary spiral is one of the most protective forms of energy that the Earth produces.

Primary spirals

Geospirals divide the lines into sections, one-half forms a spiral and the other half proceeds to the geospiral. The two halves reunite at the geospiral then proceed to the next one, where the same pattern occurs again. Spiral diameters can vary from the minimum of 2 feet (0.60 metres) to a staggering 2000 feet (609 metres) which Underwood located in Athens! Most primary spirals are left-handed from the outside to the centre and are either circular, D-shaped or oval.

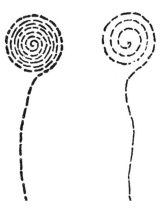

Aquastats and water lines produce 7-coiled spirals or multiples of that number. Track line spirals have three and a half coils or multiples of that number.

In the Old Religion the blind spring marked the esoteric and spiritual centre of the monument and primary spirals bestowed the site with divine protective sanctity.

Interacting and locating primary spirals

You can locate a primary spiral at the near centre of any sacred site, such as a stone circle, medicine wheel, long barrows and solitary standing stones.

Newgrange in Ireland has numerous primary spirals converging close to its geospiral centre that undoubtedly inspired its world-famous triple spiral pattern which is carved onto a stone. Holy lines run along the axis suggesting its primary function was a healing and spiritual centre, far removed from its secondary function as a burial chamber housing burial deposits.

Ring of Brodgar Orkney,
on the outside of the stone circle
there is an energetic vortex point

CHAPTER 7
Earth springs – vortex energy

Vortex energy is found within sacred precincts. 'Vortex' is a popular geomantic term used to describe a powerful form of earth energy. We have spent many years studying the effects of vortex energy in ceremonial landscapes and temple spaces. Our findings reveal how it can cleanse, revitalize and assist in the healing process.

Vortex energy

Vortices can be compared to a fresh water spring. Mineral rich, the underground water emerges alive and full of energy, creating a bubbling and babbling surface spring. Vortices are similar and can be likened to an earth spring but instead of water rising from the earth, you get energy. This type of earth spring or vortex is said to be 'electric'. Another type of vortex is said to draw energy into the earth and this is called a 'magnetic' vortex. Electric and magnetic are geomantic terms and do not relate to any form of electricity or magnetic qualities in the land. Most vortices are energizing, giving us a boost, and, as we shall soon see, they emit large quantities of negative ions.

Sedona

Sedona in the United States is world-famous for its powerful vortex energy. Native Americans considered vortices sacred and treated them as holy places. The dramatic red rock canyonlands are home to some of the most powerful vortices in the Western United States which have attracted spiritual pilgrims for millennia. Long before the Spanish arrived in the Rio Verde valley pilgrimages to Sedona were made from all over the continent from Northern Canada and Central America. Although I have yet to visit and interact with Sedona's vortex energy and so feel I cannot write about them with any personal authority or knowledge, I had the privilege of taking Mark Griffon of

SedonaMysticalTours.com around Stonehenge, Avebury and Glastonbury. Mark works intimately with Sedona's energies and shared his knowledge of vortex energy. He has been living in Sedona since 1993 and told me that vortex energy can be life changing and can help you find your divine purpose in life. Many who walk the lands of Sedona with him sense the deep heart-felt connection he has with it. Mark was a nuclear engineer whilst serving in the navy, and today he offers life readings and vision quests amid the vortices. I guess you could say that Mark is used to working with all different types of powerful energy from nuclear to vortex! I learnt a great deal from Mark and through his eyes see Sedona as a place of healing, a library of universal knowledge, where changes can occur born of deep understanding.

Electric and magnetic vortex power

An inspiring book that I read many years ago by Bernyce Barlow, *Sacred Sites of the West*, (Llewellyn Publications 1997), describes her work with vortex energy and traumatized children. Her work is truly amazing and illustrates how vortex energy facilitates emotional healing. During her therapy work she uses vortex energy to 'stir up the subconscious in order to bring it to the conscious surface.' Bernyce noticed that some vortices can amplify emotions and so she arranges overnight camps close to magnetic vortices which encourage strong dreams. She also recalls a small magnetic vortex in San Dimas Canyon, California, that 'settled the kids down'. Electric vortices, says Bernyce, can create a soothing environment for releasing emotional pain. She also points out that Burney Falls, Mount Shasta, California, creates lateral vortex energy which promotes feelings of well-being.

Avebury and Stonehenge

Geodetic spirals create electric vortex energy which will cause a dowsing rod to spin wildly. Leys, and some dragon line crossing points, invariably produce magnetic vortex energy as they draw the energy into the ground.

My late father located several electric vortices that were incorporated into sacred sites such as Avebury Henge, Stonehenge and Carnac, France, and he called these 'power points'. One power point is located along the West Kennet Stone Avenue which is a processional way linking Avebury's stone circles to another stone circle one and a half miles (2.41 kilometres) away, called the Sanctuary. One of the avenue stones is sited by a powerful vortex which, if you stand above it, is an incredible experience. You feel like you are being bathed and cleansed in pure energy. The vortex cleanses, purifies and strengthens your auric field and physical body. Another power point is located close to two megaliths called the 'Longstones' which are the lone survivors of Avebury's Beckhampton Stone Avenue and Cove feature. These cleansing points are vital and prepare you for the sacred inner circles and their powerful frequencies. Likewise, Stonehenge has a power point sited along its avenue.

The West Kennet Stone Avenue, Avebury   *Photograph Busty Taylor*

Pure water emits violet energy, water that contains iron
dowses red and hard water tends to dowse yellow.
Rank polluted waters dowse grey or black.
Agricultural chemicals can make river water grey.
If we could see the harmonic colour we would be horrified.

Swallowhead Springs close to Silbury Hill
varies in colour emissions.

Photograph Busty Taylor

CHAPTER 8
Colour dowsing – a hidden rainbow world

Dragon hills

Throughout the ancient world leys and earth energies were regarded as a living, breathing, elemental force generated by Mother Earth. The energy of the earth is yin, pushing ever upwards, giving nourishment to all things. Geomancy teaches that earth energy rises from deep within the Earth and can fill mountain peaks. Thus mountain and hillside ranges were seen as the main conductors of powerful earth energy that continuously imbue the dragon lines and smaller lines that branch off like veins flowing into the countryside.

Certainly, mountain ranges can produce dramatic effects due to localized electromagnetic fields. For instance, electric sparks rising upwards from elevated gypsum dunes in White Sands National Monument in New Mexico, occurred when a thunderstorm passed over it. Striking light rays are seen during dry spells bursting from the Andes Mountains; similar lights and mysterious glows are also seen in the Swiss Alps, and Mount Omei in China is famous for the Wenshu Lights.

The Andes lights
Mountains are seen as the main conductors of Earth energy. Pyramids were constructed to mimic nature

To ensure the undisturbed flow of energy the whole of China was systematically mapped with temple complexes and pyramids placed to collect and disperse the dragon's cosmic breath. Throughout the ancient world geomantic scientists utilized the terrestrial flows which undoubtedly produced free energy.

More than that, energy lines were seen to emit a dominant colour, a resonant frequency, and were interpreted by its particular astrological character. Understanding the localized flow, how it is affecting the area, plant growth, personal health and well-being is essential, as some lines are uplifting and elevating whilst others are enervating and will deplete the body of energy.

Planetary correspondences

Various parts of the Earth and localized regions each fell under a particular planetary influence. Other correspondences link the planets with certain parts of the body, colours, herbs, crystals and with the fortunes of men and women. Hills and mountains exert a powerful influence upon the dragon line's temperament and the shape and appearance were assigned a planetary correspondence.

Hill and mountain shapes

Mercury low and dome shaped – mentally stimulating, good for communication and mental or magical activity. Deities: Thoth, Mercury, Hermes, Loki.

Venus high and rounded – emotionally stimulating and nurturing. Promotes creative activity and can stimulate wealth. Yin energy. Wealth, banking, farming. Soothing. Deities: Venus, Aphrodite, Isis, Athena.

Mars steep sided with sharp peaks – promotes energy levels, active, courage, yang energy. Speeds up energy; energizing. Deities: Castor and Pollux.

Jupiter those with a broken (or flatter) top – promotes an optimistic nature. Productive, expansive, powerful, abundance. Deities: Jupiter, Zeus, Odin.

Saturn flat summit – responsibility, organisational skills, but can be restrictive. Deities: Cronus, Saturn.

Are there any outstanding hills or mountains in your locality? If so, what planetary influence do they exert? Geomancers learn to 'read' the landscape and interpret its innate power. Modern cityscapes can also produce height and shape which can likewise be interpreted. In the City of London's main financial district stands the 'Gherkin', a steep-sided towering skyscraper dominating the skyline. Its penetrating Mars energy symbolises the male dominance in the district. In medieval times the ground once housed a church dedicated to St Mary the Virgin and the feminine principle.

Colour dowsing

Once the major planetary influence of the locality is recognized the line's polarity, colour and frequency can be interpreted.

Popular throughout Europe is the discipline of *High Frequency Colour dowsing (HFC)* which identifies the colour, frequency and polarity of any Earth energy adding a new dimension to dowsing and geomancy. HFC can interpret the effects of an energy line on living organisms such as humans, animals and plants. Pioneers of HFC dowsing were Leon Chaumery, a French researcher, and two physicists, Antoine de Belizal and Philip Morel. Their experimental studies into the colour and nature of earth energies are legendary, as Chaumery's premature death was caused by them. Their seminal findings were not idiosyncratic to an individual preference, or subjective bias, but based on an experimental process that can easily be reproduced.

The experiment

If you place a wooden sphere on an independent support in the Earth's magnetic field there are automatically 12 different colours that can be detected with a pendulum which are always oriented in the same sequence in the Earth's magnetic field – aligning to the same compass direction. Nine of the colours are part of the visible electromagnetic spectrum, and two 'colours' are invisible – ultraviolet and infrared.

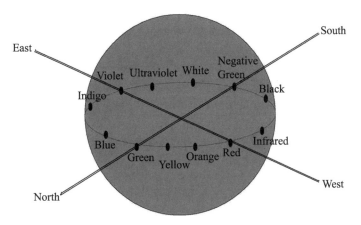

Chaumery and de Belizal's experiment

Chaumery and de Belizal discovered another invisible earth radiation which they called *negative green*. Experimental studies revealed it has two distinctive polarities, one aspect being exceptionally beneficial, the other highly toxic, and long-term exposure to the latter is severely detrimental to health. Chaumery and de Belizal developed devices that could artificially create and amplify negative green frequencies. Using one device Chaumery made an object so full of negative green that when he came to take a measurement he was instantly killed on the spot. One week later he was found in his laboratory completely mummified with no smell and no fermentation.

After Chaumery's death de Belizal collaborated with Morel to fully understand negative green's hidden properties. A breakthrough revealed that negative green's *horizontal energy waves* are positive whilst the *vertical energy waves* are intensely negative. Negative green is the strongest form of earth energy which they believed to be the cause and the cure of cancer. It is at the core of all energy centres in the human body and within the earth. In the 1960s a French researcher used a Chaumery and de Belizal pendulum to withdraw the life force – negative green – from several snails until they died or went into suspended animation. By manipulating the pendulum the snails, whose life force was suspended, were restored to life. Negative green is the most powerful force of Nature.

Dr Ibrahim Karim inherited Chaumery's research papers and documents and is a world authority on negative green. Dr Karim is an architect and expert dowser who designs hospitals, hotels and other buildings which incorporate certain shapes that promote harmonious earth radiations. Extensive research showed that the pyramid and certain dome shapes produce negative green radiation which acts as a carrier wave likened to a radio wave that carries sound information. According to Dr Karim *this vibrational quality has strong communicative properties which facilitates resonance with spiritual realms in prayer or when saying mantras.* Thus negative green acts like a portal entrance to the spiritual realms and a gateway to higher consciousness. Dr Karim noted that in spiritual energy fields the vertical inharmonious field is absent and only the harmonious horizontal aspect of negative green can be found. His seminal research into negative green and shapes which negate the side effects of drugs will prove an invaluable aspect of future health care.

Most animals shy away from negative green locations but cats, strangely, are attracted to them. Stinging nettles thrive on negative green energy and an isolated clump in open ground will, invariably, indicate a negative green location.

Earth's colours

Esoteric teachings state that all 12 earth-colours are present in each chakra, but one specific dominant colour is essential in supporting the opening of a particular chakra. For example, the dominant colour of the base chakra is red and the dominant colour of the throat chakra is blue. Likewise, earth energies contain all 12 colours but have one dominant colour which can be easily identified. Colour analysis of the Mary earth energy current at Avebury Henge illustrates this fact. Mary's dominant colour is blue which flows through the centre of the current; however, all of the earth colours are present. Many years after our colour analysis of energy lines, our work was confirmed by the research findings of Harry Oldfield who developed a camera lens that captures earth energy. The lens and photographs reveal that earth energy contains all of the colours of the electromagnetic spectrum, as did our dowsing.

	Black	
	Infra-red	
	Red	
	Orange	
	Yellow	
	Green	
Blue Mary's dominant colour	Indigo	**Blue Mary's dominant colour**
	Violet	
	Ultra-violet	
	Green	
	Yellow	
	Orange	
	Red	
	Infra-red	
	Black	

All 12 earth colours are present in an earth current, although one dominant colour prevails. Dowsing analysis by Dennis Wheatley 1990.

Earth energies which manifest the lower frequencies of red, orange, infrared, yellow, green (and some blues) are typically more earthbound, likened to energies running on the surface of the Earth. In contrast, the higher frequencies, such as blues, white, ultraviolet, indigo and violet can link mountain peaks through the air.

Colour interpretation of an energy line is simple. All that is required is a pendulum and an HFC dowsing aid which is shown in the following illustration.

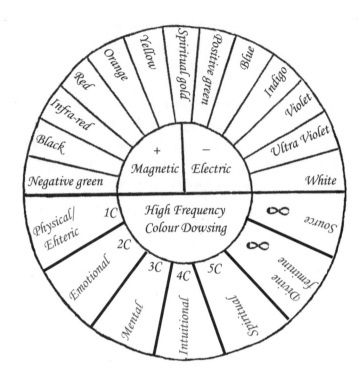

The circular dowsing aid contains a spectrum of the 12 traditional earth colours with the additional colour of spiritual gold. Two sectors identify the polarities of *magnetic* and *electric*. In the lower sector there are seven segments representing a scale of ascending frequencies from 1C to the infinite which correspond to the seven planes of spiritual consciousness and the various subtle bodies of the aura.

Polarities

The two polarities determine whether the energy has a magnetic or an electric quality. Magnetic/positive is elevating, whereas electric/negative is enervating. The polarity affects the energy field of living organisms such as humans, animals and plants. Long-term exposure to a negative/electric polarity will drain the physical body of energy and weaken the immune system. Plant growth will be stunted and animals shy away from it.

Frequency – 1C to the infinite

The frequency section extends from 1C to the infinite. So what does this mean? 'C' represents the speed of light. European dowsers use multiples of light's speed to express high dimensional frequencies. But, you may question, in Albert

Einstein's special theory of relativity, the speed of light is a universal constant, the ultimate limiting velocity, so how can we talk of 2C or 5C? A frequency of, say, 5C is simply five times that of 1C. There are higher spiritual realms which vibrate much faster than the speed of light. Some years ago physicists at Oxford University and Cal-Tech in the USA discovered a wave-particle known as the 'tachyon' which travels faster than the speed of light. So C is no longer regarded as the cosmic limiting velocity. The 'infinite' frequency is another shorthand way of expressing a frequency significantly higher than 5C.

Physical and superphysical realms

David Ashe and Peter Hewitt in their book *The Science of the God* see the speed of light as not an absolute universal velocity but rather a dividing line between physical and superphysical realities demarcating the natural from the supernatural. The tachyon concept indicates that there is more to the universe than the existence of space, matter and light, and there are what could be regarded as highly refined super-energy realms co-existing with what we regard as solid reality. But even this reality of apparent solidity has long been regarded in yoga as *maya*, the great cosmic illusion born of the senses. Einstein underpinned this when he showed that matter was, in effect, energy related by light's speed in his equation: energy = mass x the speed of light squared [$E=MC^2$].

The speed of light, in the physical universe of our senses, appears to be a limiting velocity, but what of the tachyon and the other realms of super-energy? Ashe and Hewitt posit other realms of super-energies, each having its own critical, limiting velocity in terms of multiples of light's speed, C. Each critical velocity represents a boundary between increasingly refined degrees of energy. These realms of super-physical energies can be likened to a set of Russian dolls, or co-existing concentric spheres.

Interpreting the colour of an energy line or pattern

There are 13 colours on the dowsing aid. According to Dr Karim white, gold and ultraviolet are high-dimensional spiritual colours corresponding to the divine realms of angels and higher spiritual beings. White and ultraviolet are healing colours which cleanse and purify the mind, body and spirit. They also have a soothing and calming influence that can balance overactive organs. Gold enhances wisdom, brings deep understanding and prosperity, as well as having an energizing effect on the body's immune system. The illustration on page 70 gives a brief interpretation of the colours and is followed by a more detailed explanation of each one.

Earth energy rises out of the ground full of vibrant colour which fills a sacred site or holy temple with unseen coloured light. Imagine that you are standing in a megalithic temple; all around you rising from deep within the ground is colour. Earth's colours silently influence the temple space and all life forms that interact within it.

The dominant colour and polarity of an energy line, pattern or flow reveals its influence on the immediate environment. We can also use the HFC aid to analyse the mineral properties of an underground stream.

Red magnetic Positive red indicates the line or Earth energy is strong, healthy and flowing vibrantly. Mineral rich red energies rise from deep within the Earth, and flow relatively close to its surface, and when this occurs the environ is radiant, strong and fertile. **Red electric** Long-term exposure to electric red will drain the land and living organisms of chi energy making the associated area unsuitable for habitation, farming and so forth. Domesticated animals stabled above electric red will soon become overly aggressive or restless. Electric red absorbs energy and often indicates that the line is sluggish or slow moving. Red energy influences the base chakra. Red stones: ruby, garnet, agate, carnelian. **Underground water** that is red on the HFC aid shows high iron content such as chalybeate springs.

Orange magnetic lines run close to the ground, radiate warmth and they are mildly stimulating. At various intervals along its course, or at a crossing point with another line, an orange line will descend into the earth and then ascend full of mineral rich properties. In countries such as Bali, rice fields are associated with orange lines or spirals as they promote fertility, grow and abundance. **Orange electric** lines are draining and absorb energy; they can potentially cause horticultural and fertility problems. Long-term exposure can cause digestive problems, mild depression and apathy. Orange energy is associated with the sacral chakra. Orange stones: amber, topaz, sunstone.

Yellow magnetic lines are healthy and vibrant. They flow harmonically across the land and are strongly influenced by the sun's movement. At sunrise they rise, energetically, to the surface, flow just beneath the ground and descend deeper into the earth at sunset. Stimulating the mental body, yellow lines are good for offices or spaces where intellectual energies are required. **Yellow electric** lines draw energy into the earth and can therefore be draining. Plant life will be stunted and people feel mentally sluggish or lazy when living above this coloured line. If such a line runs through the bedroom you won't want to get up in the morning! Yellow is associated with the solar plexus chakra. Yellow stones: citrine, topaz. **Underground water** that shows yellow reveals hard water or water containing other salts such as magnesium.

Green magnetic brings balance and harmony. It is a wonderful life-enhancing colour to live with. Green lines can cleanse the associated area of toxins or negative energy whilst stimulating regeneration and healing. Animals are attracted to green energy lines and often sleep or shelter above them. **Green electric** is mildly toxic and is therefore unsuitable for long-term habitation. Living above it can cause emotional mood swings, feelings of dissatisfaction, indifference and unhappiness. However, certain animals such as cats and gnats thrive upon it. Green is associated with the heart chakra. Green stones: emerald, jade, moss agate. **Underground water** showing green indicates that some type of mineralization, such as traces of copper, are present.

Blue magnetic lines are spiritual and will raise consciousness to a higher level. Blue is the dominate colour of the Mary line, and it is invariably associated with holy structures. Often within a medieval church, a blue line courses across the altar raising the frequency for an 'altar-ed state of consciousness'. Blue earth energy is said to enhance our ability to communicate and gives spiritual protection creating a safe environment for spiritual or psychic work. Deer follow protective blue lines in woods and through open countryside and animals in the wild perceive magnetic blue energy lines, even during the darkest nights, as if they were lit. **Blue electric** lines are agitated and tend to flow erratically, which is not ideal to live above. Long-tern exposure will encourage a wide range of unbalanced emotional feelings, such as a lack of motivation, or feelings of vulnerability. Blue is associated with the throat chakra. Blue stones: lapis lazuli, blue lace agate, sapphire. **Underground water** showing blue is normal drinking water, tap water, which is drinkable but not as good as violet or white.

Indigo magnetic is a high vibrational colour which is found in temple complexes and concentric stone circles. Some European dowsers see indigo lines as rising out of the earth which can link mountain peaks. Indigo lines emit a high spiritual frequency which can instantly raise awareness putting one in touch with the Higher Realms. Purifying any locale or space, Indigo brings a feeling of deep peace and spiritual strength. Indigo electric flows sporadically and can suddenly rise out of the ground like an adverse spike of energy. Areas associated with electric indigo produce feelings of loneliness and it puts us in touch with our greatest fears. **Electric indigo** encourages feelings of flight or fight and long-term exposure can promote paranoia. Domesticated animals that live above electric indigo can become distressed and show signs of irrational fear. Indigo is associated with the third eye chakra. Indigo stones: sodalite, amethyst.

Violet magnetic lines rise from the central crystal matrix at the Earth's core. Violet is the lightest and highest colour frequency which can rise to great heights above the surface of the Earth. Violet also pours into the crystal matrix from high celestial sources imbuing the Earth's energy system with ultra high cosmic frequencies. On a spiritual graded scale violet is third from the top, second is gold and white is first. **Electric violet** will drain the area of vital energy and attract negative astral influences creating a negative spiritual portal. Long-term exposure will weaken the immune system and deplete the area of energy. Violet is associated with the crown chakra. Violet stones: amethyst, sugalite. **Underground water** registering violet is absolutely pure water, the best spring water obtainable.

The invisible colours of the electromagnetic spectrum invariably emit only harmonic frequencies which promote healing and soothing effect.

Ultraviolet earth energy lines are healing, cleansing and will purify the mind, body, and spirit. It has a soothing and calming influence which will balance overactive organs. Ultraviolet spiral or vortex energy creates a portal entrance to higher dimensions enabling communication with angelic beings, nature devas and celestial realms.

Spiritual Gold is like an antiseptic which cleanses, soothes and heals. Where there is physical injury to the earth from well-boring, mining, fracking, oil, gas or mineral extraction, gold will speed up the healing process. Gold is a great healer for all of Gaia's kingdoms and gold lines and spirals are especially positive and healing places. Whilst walking my dog, Hunter, researcher and tour organizer Gary Evans and I once saw golden light radiating from the ground.

White contains all the colours of the rainbow; it protects, illuminates and radiates healing energy. Although pure white energy lines or spirals are rare they can be found within cathedrals and some sacred sites. Interacting with them expands the aura and is said to give the 'halo' effect around the crown chakra. **Underground water** that shows white is healing water, such as healing springs and holy wells. Or, where silver is dissolved into the water.

Black is not a colour. True black is simply the absence of light. Black lines can be caused by rank stagnant underground water, or negative geodetic flows. Like the black holes of space, no light can exist in the presence of black. However, by applying love and healing light harmony can be restored to the dankest and darkest lines. **Underground water** showing grey is polluted or water that contains lead. Black indicates chronic geopathic stress and will seriously affect the health of individual's living above it.

Using the HFC aid

The dowsing aid identifies the colour and quality of an energy line or pattern revealing its foremost characteristics.

- To identify the dominant colour of an earth energy or ley place the circular aid on the palm of your hand, or on the energy line or pattern.

- Hold a pendulum over the centre of the inner circle.

- Now give the silent command, show me the dominant colour of this energy line. The pendulum will, eventually, move into a linear swing selecting one of the colour segments.

- Repeat the procedure to establish the polarity of the energy.

- Repeat the procedure to find the frequency. Powerful energy lines often have an infinite frequency; for instance, a powerful yin line will invariably swing to Divine Feminine.

Earth colours can also be analyzed and measured with a pendulum designed by Chaumery and de Belizal called the Cone Fictive.

Earth energies and the aura

Colour dowsing reveals how living organisms are affected by ley and earth energy frequencies. Several people may live above the same energy line but each individual may respond differently. HFC dowsing reveals how the energy is influencing an individual's auric field as the subtle bodies are especially sensitive to earth energy. The physical body is surrounded by an ascending series of super-physical, concentric fields of energy. Collectively known as the aura these energy fields are defined as existing outside the physical body and are, progressively, known as the etheric, emotional/astral, mental and spiritual bodies.

The following interpretation guide describes the effects of earth energy upon the aura. Always let your intuition guide you when interpreting colour and frequency levels.

Dowsing the effects of earth energy upon the aura

- Ask the individual to hold the HFC dowsing aid.
- Tune into their auric field or touch their shoulder.
- Place a pendulum over the centre of the inner circle.
- Ask the pendulum to identify how the earth energy or ley is influencing the individual's auric field.
- The pendulum will select a section; for example, 'physical,' or 'emotional'.
- Now establish the polarity, magnetic/positive or electric/negative. With practice you will be able to ask the right question in your mind and no longer need the HFC guide. However, it is a useful tool as it encourages you to focus your thoughts.

1C Physical – the energy is affecting the physical body. Magnetic – positively – increasing energy levels, boosting the immune system and giving the body harmonic energy. Electric – negatively – will drain the physical body of energy and lower the immune system. Physical highs and lows.

2C Emotional/astral body – will affect the emotions. Magnetic – positively – will make you feel emotionally balanced and stable. Encourages meaningful dreams or waking visions. Uplifting. Electric – negatively – may make a person suffer from mood swings, bouts of melancholy, depression or apathy. Poor sleep. Emotional highs and lows.

3C Lower Mental body – will affect you mentally. Magnetic – positively – sharp and discerning thought processes, you can think clearly and analytically. Memory sharp and active. Strong intellect. Electric – negatively – may make a person feel mentally sluggish or slow; poor memory, indecisive and mentally fickle. Mental highs and lows.

4C Higher Mental body – intuitional – will affect you on a sensitive and psychic level. Magnetic – positively – will boost your intuition and sensitivity. Latent psychic talent will surface, develop and expand. Highly creative. Meaningful dreams and visions. Electric – negatively – may make a person feel insecure, poor judgement, intuition is blocked. Does not follow instinct or intuition, hence a sense of frustration and confusion.

5C Spiritual Angelic and devic realms – your higher auric field. Magnetic – positively – can connect you to the higher angelic realms and devic kingdoms. Also, can indicate spiritual, angelic or celestial guides are close and willing to communicate. Spiritual wisdom, enhanced perception and deep understanding. Electric – negatively – indicates a temporary block to the higher realms, or feelings of apathy, over-concern with material issues which block spiritual growth.

Infinite frequency Divine Feminine – Gaia Symbolizes the divine violet flame putting you in touch with the feminine within, and the Earth Spirit. Magnetic – positively – empathy, sensitivity, oneness with the natural world and the desire to nurture. Deep spiritual wisdom. Unconditional love. Gratitude for life on all levels. Electric – negatively – suggests a temporary block with the feeling side of your nature, or you may have a poor self-image and need to realise that you are a divine and beautiful child of Gaia.

Infinite frequency Source – Divinity – Pure energies, a spiritual portal. Magnetic – positively – puts you in touch with Source, a feeling of oneness with all that was, is and will be. Unconditional love for all. Spiritual enlightenment and wisdom. Electric –negatively – a sense of fear is blocking your path, look within, you need to love and honour yourself and realise that you are born of Heaven and Earth. Honour, love and trust your own divinity.

Yew trees grow above geospirals which emit colour and frequency.

CHAPTER 9
Harmonizing energies

Living above inharmonious energies

As we have just seen, not all earth energies are benign and living above inharmonious energy will cause health issues. Therefore, knowing how to harmonize harmful energy emissions and toxic geodetic flows is an essential part of a geomancer's tool kit. Some dowsers advocate moving an adverse energy line should it course through a property, although doing so simply moves the problem elsewhere. More importantly, Gaia chooses where she wants her energy lines to flow and her evolving energy system is billions of years ago old serving all life forms on the planet. An energy line that is disadvantageous to a human being may be advantageous to other life forms. We suggest a gentle and non-invasive healing system which does not move or disturb this ancient and delicate eco-system. Nor do I agree with the dowsing method that drives a metal stake into an underground stream or a black ley to negate its harmful frequencies. Staking Gaia as if she were a ghoulish vampire is not the way forward and it is simply not necessary.

An effective and gentle way to negate inharmonious lines is to apply colour healing. The process begins by communicating with the energy line and asking it which colour is required to harmonise the section of the line associated with the property; the rest of the line can be left to run its course as nature intended. Remain mindful that the line may be beneficial to other life forms or energies. To harmonize an energy line you need to identify its course. An energy line or current will normally enter and exit a property at two points, although a meandering current may produce more than one entry/exit point. These points are essential in the harmonizing process and they are established by using *directional dowsing* and the *show me* technique.

Finding the entry and exit points

- Establish if the property is associated with an adverse energy flow.

- Imagine or sense that your entire body and aura is surrounded by a beautiful and resplendent golden light. You are radiant and protected within the splendour of this iridescent light.

- Stand in the near-centre of the property. Hold a single dowsing rod and ask the rod to *show you the entry point of the inharmonious energy flow.*

- The rod will waver and eventually point to a particular direction.

- Follow the rod until it swings into the 'found' position.

- Establish the width by walking across it at a right-angle.

- Repeat the exercise to locate the exit point and check its width *(Alternatively, you can walk around the outside of the building to establish the entry and exit points).*

- Track the energy line to establish its course and relationship within the property.

- Establish the directional flow of the line. This is easy to do. Hold a single dowsing rod and ask to be shown the directional flow of the line. The rod will waver and point to a given direction showing you the flow's direction.

- Is the energy flow affecting plant life in the garden? Have a look around. How does the area feel?

- Find out if there are any other entry and exit points associated with the energy flow.

Harmonic colour healing

I have pioneered 'harmonic colour healing', which is safe, gentle and effective as it works in harmony with nature using colour, crystals, visualization and water to restore purity, harmony and balance. Each colour is a manifestation of the vibratory rate of a particular colour ray which has certain qualities. Colour healing is rooted in antiquity; it was used in ancient Egypt and was attributed to Thoth, patron god of physicians and scribes. Psychologists are fully aware of the power of colour, and research in America showed that when violent prisoners were placed in a pink-toned room they calmed down within ten minutes. Corporate companies use colour in consumer packaging to increase sales and restauranteurs use colour combinations to encourage relaxation.

Fast-food chains have spent large sums of money on colour analysis to promote sales and discovered that orange promotes sales and brown stimulates an earthly need to enjoy the sensual pleasure of eating. Like sound octaves colour penetrates everything it touches; ultraviolet and infrared rays are used in exactly the same way for treatments. Projection of colour as a healing tool is now increasingly accepted. Its main premise is simple: colour waves penetrate every level of existence right down to the cellular level and this is why colour has such a powerful effect. Colour is a dynamic force of nature which can change a mood, stimulate the mind and heal a wound.

Establishing the harmonic healing colour

Healing and restoring balance to an adverse energy line is straightforward. Use the HFC dowsing aid to ask the energy line which harmonic colour will harmonize the section of the line that flows through the property so that living organisms (people, animals, plants etc.) are unaffected by it. The pendulum will select a colour. The harmonic colour will raise the frequency of the energy line and restore balance.

Harmonic colour healing acknowledges the age-old principle of sympathetic magic which states that everything in the universe has its correspondence. For example, the planet Jupiter equates to the human organ of the liver, to the colour blue, to Thursday, to a particular herb, crystal, musical note, sign of the zodiac, chakra and so forth. Harmonic colour healing uses a crystal that corresponds to the divined colour. Let us say the colour selected is blue, then blue crystals are used. To harmonize the line, place a blue-coloured crystal at the entry and exit points. I, and other dowsers, use small coloured gemstones which are ideal. Dowsing will establish where to place the crystals for maximum protection and benefit.

Visualization

In addition to using crystals we also use visualization and harmonic healing water. In a quiet moment sit near the energy line and visualize the line as flowing and scintillating with the harmonic colour. See the width and length of the line filled with radiant colour; include the garden if plant life is suffering. Visualize the colour flowing in harmony with the energy line's natural directional flow – from the entry point to the exit. Now fill the entire room with the harmonic healing colour. If other rooms are affected, for instance the bedrooms, repeat the process in each room. Alternatively, visualize the entire house being filled with the resplendent all-healing harmonic colour. You can always ask the higher forces of the universe to assist you during the visualization or call upon angelic assistance. This visualization is especially effective in treating underground yang streams as the underground water will memorize and retain the projected colour.

Colleagues have successfully harmonized energy lines by using any item that contains the chosen harmonic colour. One lady harmonized an adverse line which entered her home beneath the lounge window by placing glass bowls and curtains of the harmonic colour above the line!

Harmonic healing water

Water has memory. Harmonic colours can be used to imbue water with healing power. The water is used to cleanse inharmonious earth energies and to flush out toxins within the physical body. Many years ago I began to experiment with colour and water and coined the phrase *harmonic healing water* (bear in mind I have several planets in Pisces!). You can use the divined colour to make harmonic healing water for cleansing the energy line. Place a corresponding colour crystal into a thin glass bowl containing spring or mineral water for a minimum of 20 minutes (or dowse for the correct time duration). If possible, place the bowl in the sun's warming rays. Alternatively, you can use a piece of coloured card and place the glass bowl containing the water upon it. After the allotted time remove the crystal or coloured card and sprinkle the water at the entry and exit points, as well as along the line in harmony with the energy line's natural directional flow. If a client's energy is low or has been affected by living above the adverse energy, I recommend harmonic colour water for the client to drink, to flush out toxins and to restore energy levels; likewise for garden plants and domestic animals. Just use the HFC aid to divine the best harmonic colour for the client.

Allow the colour healing to 'settle in' and then use the HFC dowsing aid (or ask a dowsing instrument) to ascertain if the energy line is harmonic by reading the line's polarity which, if harmonized, will be magnetic and life enhancing.

Spirit release

Ask a dowsing instrument if there are any other inharmonious energies associated with the property or garden, such as an earthbound spirit, negative emotional energy, or negative thought forms that require harmonizing. Home in on where the energy is by dowsing each room. When the inharmonious energy is located simply communicate with it, be that a spirit or stagnant emotional energy, and find out which colour will allow the energy to be lovingly released into the light – the full spectrum of colour. Emotional energy – past or present – may influence the colour harmonics of a room. Let us say the divined colour harmonic of the living room was electric red. This colour represents an imprint of inharmonious emotional energy. The occupants probably experience regular petty arguments and disagreements that suddenly surface causing yet more unbalanced emotional energy to prevail. The dominant electric colour attracts inharmonious energy which unconsciously influences the occupants.

Colour naturally raises the frequency so it does not matter what type of energy you are harmonizing. I do not analyze the energy I just aim to raise its frequency. I speak quietly to energies and offer love and understanding and as colour penetrates everything with divine light it has extraordinary power. We are colour light beings living amid a colourful world. Healing the land with the strong earth colours is natural, safe and very effective. As you are working with the Earth Mother's colour energies it is very empowering.

Map dowsing

Another successful way to colour harmonize a home is to draw a map of your house and commune with each room asking for its *dominate colour* and ascertain its polarity – *electric or magnetic*. You will see unfold before your eyes the once hidden colours silently influencing the room. Use your own sensitivity to guide you. The rooms that require harmonizing with instantly become apparent. Now walk around each room sensing where the energy feels strongest and dowse for the harmonic colour. The initial map dowsing and questioning probably reflects your experience of physically divining the room. Ask if there are any other negative frequencies which require colour harmonizing and harmonize each room until it is free of inharmonious energy. Have fun as healing is uplifting and does not have to be 'heavy' and always use psychic protection prior to harmonizing which is explained in the following chapter.

The harmonic colour spectrum that Gaia emits is all healing. Colours such as pink or purple variations such as magenta are absent because they can be created by a mix of multiple wavelengths. Colours containing only one wavelength are called by academics 'pure colours' and these equate to the earth colours. Visible wavelengths of colour can pass through the Earth's atmosphere. A beautiful and simple example of this phenomenon is that clean air scatters blue light more than red wavelengths and so the midday sky appears blue.

Many species can see light with frequencies outside the human visible spectrum. Bees and many other insects can detect ultraviolet light which helps them find nectar in flowers. Plant species that depend on insect pollination owe reproductive success to their appearance in ultraviolet light rather than how colourful they appear to humans. Birds, too, can see into ultraviolet and some have sex-dependent markings on their plumage that are visible only in the ultraviolet range. Many animals that can see into the ultraviolet range cannot see red light or any other reddish wavelengths. For example, a bees' visible spectrum ends just before the orange wavelength begins.

Spiritualize your home

Knowing the dominant colour of a room can help explain why an individual behaves in a particular manner as they are unconsciously responding to the colour harmonics. Some children instantly dislike a room and their behaviour can become emotional or challenging in a particular environment. Children are exceptionally sensitive to the earth colours. When I first moved into the house where I am currently living, I naturally resonated with the land energies. However, after about 6 months I realized that I spent a lot of my time daydreaming and imagining situations, feeling good but achieving little. I colour divined my home and discovered the dominate, or ruling colour, was violet which is a high chakra and inspirational colour. A highly creative colour which is the colour of poets, musicians, artists and writers as they can reach up to a higher dimension and pull down what they see. However, the polarity was electric. At first I thought the divined polarity was the wrong answer, however, it explained my day dreaming fantasies. I realised that I needed to ground the naturally occurring violet energies and make them work for me. Instead of rationalizing the situation I divined the harmonic healing earth colour which was yellow – the colour of the intellect. I began to work with the vibrational harmonics of yellow. I introduced yellow in my living room, I got up early when the sun rose (representing yellow light rays), and at some point in the day I applied a 'colour breathing' exercise which is explained later. I created an office like area and began to write from the morning until the late afternoon – staying within the parameters of yellow/sun energies. A few days later I divined the living area which was violet again, but this time it was magnetic and harmonic. Instead of daydreaming I became far more productive and the colour yellow helped to ground my inspiration. Within three months of harmonizing I was writing an astrological column for a local newspaper and had spoken on the local BBC radio about astrology. My daydreaming had ceased but the inspiration remained and instead of imagining I was a writer, I was now living my dream.

Harmonic colour healing works on so many levels. Regular colour healing enhances the property and can assist in spiritualizing our lives. Many people like to colour cleanse their homes on a regular basics, for example, at the Quarter Days at the times of the Spring Equinox March 21st – a natural time to 'spring clean', the Summer Solstice 21st June, the Autumn Equinox September 23rd and the Winter Solstice just before Christmas on December 21st. These are sacred days when the Sun reaches 0 degrees of Aries, Cancer, Libra and Capricorn respectively. Gradually extend your knowledge by furthering your studies of colour. Practice harmonizing areas within the home and garden. Your home will benefit from being bathed in colour.

Pure light and its rainbow colours are a gift from Great Spirit and the earth colours are Gaia's light spectrum emanating from deep within the earth – so let us embrace the colours of the world both seen and unseen.

The late and great Swindon based dowser and author John Farrar taught me to harmonize energy lines in 1988. John and I worked alongside one another for many years. His inventive and perceptive mind inspired me for a large part of my life and together we faced many different aspects of toxic earth energy and lost spirits. John always said *As a servant of humanity you are never alone as you attract spiritual forces that are constantly assisting and protecting you.* So very true.

Healing with the colours of the Earth

Many years ago I began to make healing essences at sacred sites using the living energies of the Earth. Positive/magnetic energy lines and geospirals are all-healing and their colour-energy can be transferred to water to make a powerful remedy.

First, you need to locate an energy line and interpret its colour and polarity; obviously, only harmonic magnetic lines are used to make remedies and never use the energies of black or negative green. Spiritual and psychic development essences can be made from the high chakra colours such as blue, indigo, violet and ultraviolet energies. Geospirals are perfect for making a healing remedy, red lines for making rejuvenating or energy-boosting remedies, and harmonic green energy is especially effective for treating emotional issues, from fear to heart ache. Always use your own intuition when making remedies. I made an excellent 'courage' remedy from a powerful red energy line that flows through a Druid ceremonial centre! My sacred site earth energy essences are listed at the back of the book and are available from my website.

Making Earth Colour Essences

Eleven earth colours are used to make the essences; infrared (especially good for clearing base chakra or deep-rooted emotional blockages from childhood or even past lives), red, orange, yellow, spiritual gold, positive green, blue, indigo, violet, ultra-violet and white. Making remedies at sacred sites or in the open countryside is a wonderful and rewarding experience. I use the 'sun method' developed by Dr Edward Bach who made the original Bach Flower Remedies. The sun method uses a thin glass bowl filled with pure water which is placed on the geospiral or energy line, preferably when the sun is shining. Determine the time duration by dowsing or leave for a minimum of 20 minutes. A 3-minute duration is all that is required when making a power point or vortex energy remedy! I always ask Gaia, the land and the energy line for permission to make the healing remedy, and then I ask for the Earth's healing energies and colour to be absorbed into the water. I meditate by the bowl and see the energy of the land spiralling into the water, filling it with love, colour and healing power. Afterwards I thank Gaia, the sun and the yin and yang powers of creation for their assistance. I then dowse the water using the HFC guide which always matches the colour energy line! It's magical!

Stock bottles

Once the energies are infused into the water add some brandy or vodka as the alcohol acts as a preservative. As a guideline, a cup of water requires a quarter of the amount of alcohol for long-term storage. I call this a 'stock bottle'. I store my stock bottle remedies in glass bottles and not plastic ones. They will last for years! You can choose to make a remedy at a new or full moon, or a particular time of the solar year, for example, May Day (Beltane) or the Summer Solstice.

Treatment bottles

Treatment bottles are the most convenient and economical way to take the remedies. A treatment bottle is a 30 millilitre (1 fluid ounce) dropper bottle which is available from most pharmacies or from stores on the internet. Fill the treatment bottle with pure non-carbonated spring or mineral water. From the stock bottle take 2-4 drops (or dowse how many drops are required) and add to the treatment bottle. If the treatment bottle is new you can use it straightaway. However, if you are reusing a bottle sterilize it first. Replace the dropper cap and screw it tight; this is your treatment bottle which will last for around 10 days. However, if you think you will need the bottle for more than 10 days, add one teaspoon of alcohol to the bottle as it acts as a preservative.

Using a treatment bottle

Dowsing will determine the dosage, when and how many times a day you should take the remedy. Alternatively, simply take four drops just below the tongue (lift up the tongue and use the dropper to place the drops beneath it), or add the drops to a glass of water and sip and take four times a day.

Remedies and the aura

Remedies can be placed into the aura. Place the remedy drops onto the palm of your hand and then rub both hands together. Now use the palms of your hand to place the remedy into the aura – from the feet, all over the body, back and front and just above the crown chakra. Dowsing can also determine which chakra or chakras will best receive the remedies for healing.

The Earth's energy system can help us in so many ways. In times of need we can turn to our Earth Mother to help heal and care for us with her living rainbow colours. Coloured energy lines and geospirals interlace the planet and so no matter where you live you can make a healing remedy.

*Buildings can retain energies
from centuries past..*

CHAPTER 10
Space clearing

Throughout ancient China it was thought that if you moved into someone else's property it was like stepping into their shoes; their energy becomes your energy, and you can take on a similar destiny, be that favourable or unfavourable. Interpreting the energy within a construct is therefore essential and the main aim is to create a healthy flow of energy. To a geomancer, whatever is seen in the home or office is a physical manifestation of the person's internal process and the processes of those with whom they live with. In other words, your personal environment is a reflection of your inner space. One way to enhance the energetic quality of the home or workspace is to *space clear*. The first step is to de-clutter your home and have a good spring-clean. Clutter blocks the free-flow of Chi energy.

> *Space clearing cleanses and purifies the atmosphere within a building and allows the chi energy to flow harmoniously.*

Feeling the unseen energy

Walk around your home, office or a friend's house and observe each room. Allow yourself to experience the emotions that arise within you as you gently become intuitively aware of what you see. If you feel negative emotions stir within, such as anger or depression, use this as your guide to interpreting the room's energetic signature. Stagnant or emotional energy can become imprinted or accumulate within a property as the walls, floors, ceilings, carpets, furniture, etc. soak up energy. All living beings, plants, animals and people, unconsciously absorb whatever has happened in a room or home, good or bad, past or present.

A property's imprinted energy releases its influence which can potentially cause future occupants to experience the same issues as those who previously lived there. For instance, if a new house was occupied by a married couple who constantly argued and eventually divorced, you can bet that the next couple to live in the house will repeat the behavioural pattern of the former occupants as the unseen emotional energy prevails. Space clearing has the power to transform the energy and restore peace and harmony.

Space clear after

- Divorces or separation.
- Arguments.
- Illness.
- Death.
- When you feel negative energies.
- Moving into a new home.
- To cleanse and energize the home.
- To transform the atmosphere of the property.
- To encourage harmony, health and good relationships.
- Clearing old, stagnant, or negative thought-forms and inharmonious emotional cycles or patterns.
- After you have de-cluttered your home or office.
- When you feel stuck either personally or professionally.
- After you have harmonized energy lines or flows.

Space-clearing techniques

One method of clearing a property is to use a Native American smudge stick made of sage. The smudge stick is lit and the smoke is waved around filling the room with its scent and the all-cleansing smoke. Alternatively you can use crystals, such as black tourmaline or a crystal wand which deflect negative energy. However, instead of wafting a smudge stick around the room you can wave a crystal around focusing on clearing away negative energy and thought vibrations. Some people use sound such as drumming to shift and clear negativity.

Removing inharmonious energy

Whether you are using a smudge stick or a crystal for space clearing, when you sense an inharmonious area gently rotate the smudge stick or crystal counter-clockwise which removes the stagnant energy and then 'put in' positive all-healing energy by making clockwise rotations. Continue to smudge/cleanse the property repeating the process of removing inharmonious energy and putting in positive all-healing and loving energy. If you wish, before smudging you can ask a dowsing instrument to show you any inharmonious areas, or just use your intuition. Pay special attention to the room's corners and the four cardinal directions of each room and the house. I close the smudging session by walking with the smudge stick north to south and east to west, forming the divine cross to protect the building and its occupants and then I seal my work. One way to seal the space clearing is to visualize a large infinity symbol covering the room or the property. Alternatively, visualize the symbol at the centre of the house.

Space-clearing tips

- Prior to locating, or working with, any form of negative energy always psychically protect yourself *(see below)*.

- Set your intent – *to clear the adverse energies*.

- See the end result – *visualize the room/s clear and radiant*.

- Space clear using your chosen method – *smudge stick, crystal wand, drum, singing bowl, etc.*

- When you have finished 'seal' your work.

After space clearing people can manifest what they want in their lives and they will experience clarity, vitality, positive and creative energy.

Psychic protection

Psychic protection gives you spiritual and physical protection from inharmonious or adverse energies. Prior to any dowsing work psychically protect yourself; it only takes a few minutes and it can make a real difference to your dowsing.

- Sit down in a quiet location.

- Relax as best as you can and take a couple of deep breaths.

- As you inhale imagine that you are breathing in a beautiful golden-coloured light, and as you exhale imagine the light filling your aura. Gold is the ultimate protective colour in the physical realm; its reflective properties keep negative energies from entering your aura.

- Continue to breathe in the protective healing light until your aura is totally filled with the radiant golden light.

Threefold protection

In the Druid tradition threefold magic is all-powerful and so I created a psychic technique that has threefold protection which can be applied once your aura is filled with gold.

- Now imagine a mirror surrounding the aura which has the power to deflect and rebound all negative energy. (Second phase protection.)

- Beginning with the base chakra place a beautiful rose on the chakra point. Those in harmony with your intent and being will smell the beauty of the rose's sweet scent. Forces and energies that are not in harmony with your intent or being will sense the protective thorns warning them to go no further. (Third phase protection.)

- Nothing will penetrate this threefold protection. You are protected.

- Ask the godhead/Source to protect you and help you to help others.

Clearing with a crystal elixir

Numerous clearing remedies and sprays are on the market. I recommend an Italian crystal elixir which consists of energized water that contains numerous tiny and highly charged crystals and which I found to be one of the best energy clearing remedies on the market. All that is required is to place 21 drops of the fluid in the corners of each room of the house, the crossing points of the Curry Grid, and at the entry and exit points of a negative grid, ley or adverse current that courses though the property. For more information go to www.rei-shen-ki. it info@rei-shen-ki.it Explore different methods of clearing and find one that suits you.

Gadgets

Russian research has found that adverse grid systems, such as the Curry, Benker and Hartmann double lines or 'knots', emit higher levels of positive ions. Therefore an ionizer placed in the room containing the grid line is a great counter-measure which re-balances the ionic levels. There are numerous geopathic stress devices which are designed to negate adverse Earth energies but an old-fashioned rock-salt lamp is an ideal choice as it emits negative ions.

Making a geopathic stress diffuser

An inexpensive way of neutralizing geopathic stress is to have a Lakhovsky coil in the property. The copper coil is safe and very effective at space clearing as it negates geopathic stress emitted from leys, Earth energies, grid lines and underground water and is considered a great 'all rounder'. www.lakhovskyscoil.com describes how to make the coil.

> *A simple way of making a geopathic stress coil is to take two strips of copper wire and coil them around one another to make a circle with a diameter of approximately 20 inches (50 centimetres). Place it in the attic – it's that simple!*

New innovations

Our studies into the geospiral phenomenon show that its unique spiral shape has a profound effect upon the environment. When worn as a necklace it will reduce the impact of geopathic stress and in some cases completely negate its influence. A copper reproduction scaled to around 20 inches (50 centimetres) acts as a geopathic stress diffuser which can be placed in the home or workspace. If you wish to make one include the necklaces as two concentric circles that encase

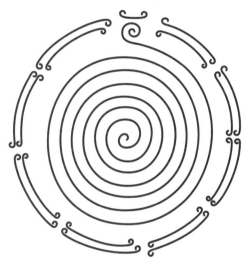

the spiral pattern and make sure the smaller spiral is orientated towards the underground stream or the most powerful line to be diffused. Use information dowsing to ascertain if the spiral should be counter-clockwise or clockwise. Nature's healing geospiral is a great antidote for geopathic stress. It is especially effective for transforming underground yang water and black leys or impure water. Geospiral pendants can be bought from my website.

Long Meg stone circle in the Lake District is one of the largest stone circles in England.

The tall stone is called Long Meg and its energy field is intense.

CHAPTER 11
Aura readings

Clairvoyants and sensitives see a healthy aura as scintillating colours which surround the physical body. When we are ill, or about to become ill, our aura may appear dull or show grey patches. Psychics have noted that our thoughts and emotions such as anger and jealously can influence and be identified within the auric field. Auras often have a dominant colour; for instance, a dominant red auric colour reveals a passionate person with high energy levels. However, if it is dark red or tinted with grey, it suggests unbalanced emotions such as anger, or an emotional issue needs to be addressed. For those that cannot see auric colours dowsing reveals the aura's dominant colour and ascertains if it is a harmonic or an inharmonious colour – like the dark-coloured or grey areas that psychics see – as well as detecting spirit guide energy.

Aura colour dowsing is very accurate and an aura reading can provide valuable insight into a person's life. When I give workshops and lectures at events such as the Mind, Body, Spirit Experience many of the participants have an aura photograph taken. When I dowse their aura it is always the same, or similar to, the dominant colour as seen in the photograph.

Auric colour dowsing

- Make contact with the person, animal or plant, etc., for instance, touch their shoulder or arm with one hand.

- Hold a pendulum over the central white area on the colour dowsing aid. Give the gentle command, *show me the dominate colour of this person's aura*. The pendulum will select one of the colours.

- Check the polarity of the colour. Magnetic indicates a vibrant and bright colour and an electric polarity a dull or unbalanced colour.

- If the polarity is negative/electric ask the pendulum to *show the harmonic healing colour which will restore balance to this person's auric field*.

Aura readings

Let us imagine the pendulum showed blue as the dominant colour and the polarity was magnetic/positive. This would show that the person is very sensitive and intuitive. Blue indicates a patient, caring nature and the ability to work alongside others. Blue in the aura also suggests spirituality, wisdom and the ability to teach or assist others. Interests may include holistic or complementary medicine or just as likely working in teaching, communication or the caring profession.

Harmonic healing colours

If you dowse the aura and the colour is negative/electric a healing colour is required to restore balance and harmony to the aura. Once the pendulum has selected a healing colour the person can wear the colour, carry crystals of that colour or use a colour breathing visualization technique to restore harmony. Also, a harmonic colour water remedy can be made and taken which will re-establish energy levels and flush out toxins. *(See chapter 9 for details).*

Colour breathing visualization

- *Sit down in a quiet and comfortable location.*
- *Relax as best as you can and take a couple of deep breaths.*
- *Imagine an infinite cloud of the harmonic healing colour just in front of you.*
- *As you inhale, imagine that you are breathing in the beautiful, all-healing colour, and as you exhale imagine the colour filling your aura.*
- *Continue to breathe in the harmonic healing colour until your aura is filled with the radiant colour.*

Interpreting the aura colours

Red is a strong physical colour which can stimulate energy, vitality, regeneration of the cells, blood and tissue, and it is a hot colour which generates heat and warmth. Red is the colour of empowerment, action and shows healthy energy levels. It is the colour of new beginnings and adventures therefore red in the aura brings change – a new chapter in life is about to unfold. Red represents all things physical and materialistic thinking and indicates the individual likes to be active and has leadership qualities. Red is the colour of activity, it rules the emotional body, and is the colour of our sexuality, fear and anger. Red can represent passion and it is no coincidence that many bars and nightclubs use red lavishly in their décor. Red often indicates our struggle with attachments on the physical plane or signifies emotional energy. Red encourages us to take full responsibility for everything that happens in our lives. A red personality is a leader, adventurer and initiator of ideas and a person who enjoys life to the full. Red opens the Root (Muladhara) chakra to release a powerful current of energy that surges through the core of our Being. **Electric Red** shows that you are highly emotional, passionate and may be overwhelmed by an emotional issue – past or present. In the aura it indicates that you should face a fear as it is holding you back. Your energy levels may fluctuate as well as your moods. You have leadership skills, yet you are currently feeling inferior. You may be experiencing a sense of frustration as electric red in the aura signifies a block. The harmonic healing colour will encourage balance and regeneration on all levels.

Infrared (crimson red) Crimson red in the aura is the colour of the Seer, someone that is gifted with second sight. You are highly psychic and intuitive. You are sensitive to the suffering of others and would make an excellent medium or healer. **Electric infrared** Although you are highly psychic you are not listening to the feeling side of your nature and therefore it is blocked. Fear may be at the root cause and you need to realise that a positive attitude is beneficial to your future. The harmonic healing colour will encourage you to go beyond fear and it gently dissolves blockages allowing us to see our future with inner strength and integrity.

Orange is sunlight, warmth and fire. It is a balanced mix of red – physical – and yellow – mental. In the aura it provides the energy to overcome a problem or an illness and the enthusiasm to accomplish far-reaching goals. Orange is a transitional colour which brings change and growth which leads to abundance. Orange is good for the heart and provides a boost of energy when tired or fatigued. Psychologically, it generates wakefulness and activity. Wear orange if you need a boost of energy! You are bold and courageous with orange! Orange is a wonderful colour for balancing the emotional body and the digestive system. It promotes the assimilation of food and events in one's life; it literally helps us to digest life. It also helps to integrate what we need to accept and releases what is no longer appropriate, whether this is a frame of mind, bad habit, job or a person. Orange is good at releasing self-pity, lack of self-worth and unwillingness to forgive. An orange personality is warm, caring and sympathetic (a nurse for example), but needs to learn to be self-reliant and not depend on other people's approval in order to function. Orange encourages personal power, opens the Sacral (Svadhisthana) chakra and provides us with courage. **Electric Orange** in the aura suggests that you are stuck in a rut and unable to grow. You may feel that life has grounded to a halt and feel unable to move forward. This may be echoed in the physical body as a sluggish digestive system or a general lack of vitality – even a sense of apathy. You may be holding onto feelings such as resentment, guilt or fear and need to simply let go of any inner anger. The harmonic healing colour will help to restore your physical energies and wear orange!

Yellow represents the intellect. Someone with yellow in their aura has the power to inspire new ideas and manifest them through speech and positive action. Yellow also purifies the immune system which leads to a long productive life. On a spiritual level yellow brings hope for all of humanity, and on a practical level yellow can assist in logical problem solving. Yellow will bring answers to problems. A person with dominate yellow is usually positive and inspiring with a warm and loving nature. A yellow person is generally a good organizer, intellectual, efficient and good at coping with structure, and therefore would be good at management or law, but needs to be careful that the mind does not manage the heart. Yellow opens the Solar Plexus (Manipura) chakra and encourages us to focus with intention until we find a positive solution. **Electric yellow** indicates you may be struggling to find a solution to a problem. Your mental faculties may be sluggish and you may be feeling at a low mental ebb or creatively dry and uninspired. Determine the harmonic colour which will energetically boost your mind and body.

Green is the colour of the heart, the rich and fertile lands of Gaia and it is the colour of growth which leads to a harvest – abundance. In green we are deeply rooted and appreciate all other life forms. In the aura green is the energy that sparks our imagination and creativity and signifies someone who takes great pleasure in life's simple gifts. In America green is associated with the dollar bill with slang terms such as 'greenbacks' and the 'green stuff'. The early leaders of America were Masons, a secret order and society. They made certain that the dollar bill had Masonic symbols such as the all-seeing eye on top of the pyramid. Furthermore, they knew the metaphysical properties of colour; green draws power from the universe, stimulates supply – food, cash, love and aids manifestation. Spring green in the aura indicates that a new cycle is about to unfold which can bring change, growth or a new love into our lives. A green person is usually sensitive, loving, caring and is fond of nature and gardening. The home is important to them as it represents security and comfort. However, if this is threatened they will respond will strength and power to protect themselves. Green opens the Heart (Anahata) chakra and guides us to be giving, nurturing and loving. **Electric green** indicates a blocked heart chakra and sometimes indicates a sense of loss. This could be due to challenges within a relationship or the ending of a relationship, or it can signify a stage in your life when you are mourning a loss. Often electric green appears in the aura when your life lacks something – a purpose, skill, support or love. Look within and be truthful – what does your life lack? Seek and you will find the seed of your future which just needs a little faith to breathe life into your dreams. Find the harmonic healing colour which will encourage faith, balance and growth.

Blue is one of the cool colours which is associated with an aspect of the mind which is different to yellow. It is the colour of spiritual truth and wisdom. Blue encourages us to take mental control and brings clarity, creativity and the acceptance of our responsibilities. Blue can eliminate confusion so that we can see clearly. Blue is the energy of the spiritual teacher and indicates that you are intuitive, sensitive, patient and kind. Blue is a cool and soothing colour that can relieve tension and reduce fevers. Under blue's protective energy we can find inner peace, contentment and true joy in living. If dark navy blue is present in the aura it indicates an in-pouring of spiritual knowledge from higher sources. When sky blue is present it suggests the individual is going through the student process, either studying or learning a new skill. Blue represents a person who is honest, caring and who strives to serve all those they care for. Blue can be used to restore faith in one's life and to calm an over-emotional nature. Blue opens the throat (Vishuddha) chakra and encourages us to use our voice to assist and help others and to speak the truth with quiet integrity. **Electric blue** indicates a blocked throat chakra – you may feel you cannot voice your truth or opinion on a particular matter. You may also find it difficult to fully relax and may even be experiencing a bout of insomnia. The harmonic healing colour will restore harmony and balance.

Indigo represents a deep connection with Spirit. Indigo guides us to surrender the notion that we are separate from Source, teaching us that all is one. Indigo can indicate a time of transition, bringing changes that are often foretold by a vision; therefore, it is the colour of self-awareness. Indigo silently leads you to a better future and opens new pathways to greater understanding. Indigo opens the Third Eye (Ajna) chakra and encourages us to 'see' clearly the past, present and future. **Electric indigo** often indicates a sense of confusion or the inability to see where you are going in life. You may be unsure of your direction and your usually sharp sense of intuition is temporarily blocked. Find the harmonic healing colour which will restore harmony by clearing blockages.

Violet and White White is the combined presence of all the colours creating perfect Light. White or violet in the aura shows a spiritually mature person with the gift of healing. Violet indicates psychic talent and medium skills inherited from past lives. Violet-White inspires us to choose the path of love, light, beauty and wisdom. Violet-White opens the Crown (Sahasrara) chakra making a divine connection to the infinite Universe. **Lavender** when the two high vibrational colours of violet and white are mixed lavender is created. It is the colour of a Master Energy and shows a Master or Higher Guide present in the auric field. **Electric violet/white** you have great psychic talent which you are not using and which could help to inspire others. Presently, you may be experiencing emotional highs/lows, or a lack of direction. Violet is a high vibrational colour which can take us to great heights or sometimes to extreme lows. The harmonic healing colour will help to restore any emotional, mental, or spiritual imbalance.

Ultraviolet in the aura shows that you are a highly spiritual person, have clairvoyant ability, and you are exceptionally sensitive to your surroundings. You also have the ability to heal and to walk through portals. Ultraviolet is a high dimensional spiritual colour connecting you to the divine realms of angels, higher spiritual and celestial beings. Ultraviolet is a healing colour which cleanses and purifies the mind, body and spirit. **Electric ultraviolet** shows that you are highly sensitive to the thoughts and feelings of other people which you soak up like a sponge. Although you are highly receptive to higher realms and have clairvoyant ability, you lack a sense of trust. However, once you learn to trust the universe you will find that your connection to the spiritual realm opens up a whole new level of awareness. The harmonic healing colour will assist this process.

Spiritual gold shows that you are a wise person with deep spiritual awareness; an old soul. Gold brings understanding and has an energizing effect, boosting energy levels within the physical body. Long associated with alchemy, gold is a transformative colour that can transmute lower vibrational energies into a purer state of resonance. Gold in the aura shows that you are growing spiritually and that you have the ability to commune with higher dimensions. From early childhood you probably experienced contact with higher dimensional beings, such as tree devas or fairies. Gold is cleansing and protective and lovingly connects you to your spiritual self. **Electric gold** your energy levels are probably low and you may easily tire. Make sure that you are eating a good balanced diet and getting plenty of rest. Electric gold often indicates the immune system is low or your body may have a mineral deficiency. The harmonic healing colour will encourage the body to heal itself and restore energy levels.

Further analysis

For a holistic understanding of an individual's physical, emotional, mental and spiritual well being, dowse each layer of the auric field separately to find its dominant colour.

Guide energies

When guides are spoken of it conjures up the image of a personified being such as a wise Native American, Chinese healer, Druid magician or a Hindu sage. In the aura the *energy* of a higher being manifests as concentric circles of beautiful light. Bejewelling the aura these light spheres are positive entities that assist humankind's evolution, offer external information and helpful guidance. Granted permission by the host either unconsciously or consciously through prayer, guide energies are full of radiant and scintillating colour. Guide energy can give the impression of being predominantly male or female but most seem to have no specific sexual identity. Some seem to give off an energy field of great wisdom whilst others seem juvenile and playful!

Guide energies are generally found around the upper part of the body – from the heart chakra upwards.

Dowsing guide energy

- Make contact with the person by touching their shoulder, arm or holding their hand for a moment.

- Ascertain if they have guide energy in their auric field.

- If the answer is 'yes', choose one side of the body to dowse first. Tune into the guide energy by visualizing and sensing concentric spheres of loving light.

- Hold a pendulum and start dowsing around the heart chakra area, and then slowly and gradually extend your dowsing away from the physical body to a distance of about 2-3 feet (0.60-0.91 metres). By doing so you will be dowsing all of the subtle bodies of the aura.

- Dowse the upper part of the body front/back and sides so that the entire area surrounding the physical body/aura has been thoroughly dowsed.

- When guide energy is detected the pendulum will swing in a fast and energetic clockwise motion. Or, the pendulum will bounce.

- You may sense a loving presence.

- Check which subtle body the guide energy resides in: emotional, lower/ higher mental or spiritual body.

- Tune into the energy. Allow your mind to be open and receptive to feelings and images which will aid interpretation.

- Feel the energy with the palm of your hand – you may sense a sudden warmth. Or simply use the palm of your hand to detect guide energy.

You can use dowsing to find the directional flow of your vivaxis and when you align to your vivaxis you must be on neutral ground and away from powerful earth energies.

One of the most powerful places in Orkney is the Tomb of Beagles.

CHAPTER 12
Vivaxis - healing with earth energies

Your aura connects you to the Earth and to the place where you were born. This is a little-known fact even amongst advanced holistic practitioners. All living creatures are invisibly connected to their birthplace by a magnetic 'umbilical cord' called a 'vivaxis' – viva is Latin for life – and *axis* is a central line. This cord literally plugs you into the earth and its life-supporting energies, even if you move thousands of miles away.

During the 1960s Canadian researcher and author Frances Nixon discovered the life-changing vivaxis principle which was validated and tested by William Tiller and other leading physicists and scientists at Stanford University – yet their remarkable findings never made headline news. Many people with either mild or chronic health complaints came to Frances to reconnect to their vivaxis and they were invariably cured of their aliments. People from all over the world studied with Frances; her teachings are invaluable and no book on earth energies would be complete without her deep understanding of the Earth's subtle energies. After many years of research Frances concluded that a disturbed vivaxis can result in dis-ease and illness. However, restoring your vivaxis creates balance, harmony and promotes longevity. When I first practised connecting to my vivaxis I was amazed that I could find the direction of my birthplace with my fingertip! Connecting to your vivaxis can be an incredible experience because you are reconnecting to an invisible aspect of your being and the land upon which you were born. Personally, the process makes me feel 'whole' and on a physical level my body feels stronger, and spiritually I feel deeply reconnected to the land, the place where I incarnated.

Birth and the vivaxis

Frances discovered one of nature's most profound secrets. At the moment of birth every living creature creates a spherical wave field of rotating magnetic energy which anchors itself into its magnetic and physical location. Scientists have studied Earth's magnetic radiations which form a massive network of energy waves and currents in both horizontal and vertical directions. A growing foetus in the womb is constantly subjected to these magnetic influxes and becomes magnetized to that geophysical location. A permanent magnetic alignment is introduced into the atomic structure of the bones as they solidify and also the central nervous system, forming a magnetic two-way relationship to the magnetically-charged vivaxis. Around the time of a mother's first labour pains the baby instinctively pulls the magnetic currents and waves into a common axis or point. Incidentally, it may be this magnetizing process that induces the labour pains and when completed birthing can commence. All living creatures repeat this natural vivaxis process which may explain why certain animals, such as migrating birds and fish, automatically know how to return to their place of birth.

The two-way energy flow to the birth location remains in position for life. It is your personal etheric connection to the Earth and vice versa. The vivaxis principle is simple. It is a sphere of magnetic energy that records changes which occur within your physical, emotional and mental systems. It also receives and collects energies pulsating from the elements deep within the Earth as well as celestial influences. When a vivaxis connection is disturbed, more often than not by emotional, mental chemical, biophysical or electromagnetic energies, illness can occur. When a vivaxis is restored health is maintained and this can be achieved by doing a simple exercise.

Auric connections

The vivaxis is connected to the aura by two bands of energy, the outer and inner rims as shown in the diagram. Visualize this link as a constant communication and energy exchange between the auric bands and your vivaxis. One band is said to be gravitational and the other band is magnetic. More importantly these bands reflect the relationship of where you were born and where you live now.

The bands and altitude

If you live above your vivaxis – at a higher elevation – the outer auric band is magnetic and the inner band gravitational. If you live at an altitude below your vivaxis your outer band is gravitational and the inner band is magnetic. I live near Avebury in England but I was born in London. I can find the altitude of the two locations by doing an internet search which is given in metres or feet above sea level. For instance, the altitude of London is 104 feet (31.69 metres) and the altitude of Marlborough is 426 feet (129.84 metres). Therefore, I live

Wave links to a person's vivaxis

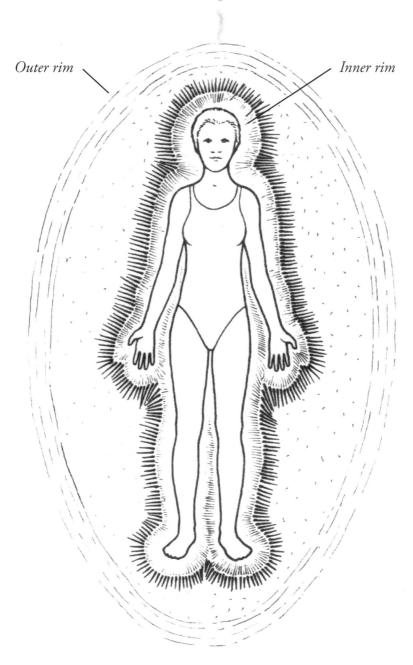

Outer rim

Inner rim

above my vivaxis, and my outer auric rim is magnetic and the inner etheric rim is gravitational. Finding whether you live above or below your vivaxis is important and you need to establish this information before you can align to your vivaxis.

The two-way energy flow

The vivaxis two-way energy flow is constant. Vivaxis energies flow towards us into the left hand and foot, and back out to the vivaxis via the right hand and foot. Energies flowing towards us from the vivaxis flow in a vertical direction up or down in altitude until reaching our present level of elevation. Then they flow in a horizontal direction until they reach the receiving hand and foot. Those standing above the altitude of their vivaxis will receive these magnetic energies through the left forefinger. Those standing below will receive the magnetic energies through the left ring finger.

Dowsing to find your vivaxis

You can find the direction of your vivaxis by dowsing the area between the two bands. However, prior to any vivaxis work Frances recommends that you need to 'neutralize' your energies first.

Neutralizing technique

The 'accordion exercise' is a neutralizing technique which prepares the mind and body for the vivaxis alignment experience. Vivaxis energies must ground unobstructed through the feet, so do this exercise barefoot, and make sure the bottom of any clothing is not touching the feet. Your heels, ankles and big toe joints should be pressed tightly together forming a closed circuit.

- Place the palms of your hands facing one another and align the whorls of the fingers of each hand.
- Slowly and with extreme pressure press the fingers together, in and out like an accordion making sure the palms do not touch.

Locating and channelling your vivaxis

Once your energies are neutralized you are ready to locate and channel your vivaxis. 'Channelling' and 'vectoring' were words that Frances used to describe tuning into your vivaxis, which is a bit like tuning into a radio station. Once tuned in you can bring the energies of the physical body into harmony with the two-way energy currents of the vivaxis. A strengthened alignment corrects any imbalances, abnormal nerve or muscle disorders and destroys foreign bodies such as bacteria or viruses. Prior to the exercises remove all headgear, jewellery, tight clothing, glasses, contact lenses, socks and shoes.

Preparing to locate your vivaxis

- Do not locate or channel for at least 20 minutes after eating.
- Do not locate or channel at the new or full moon; wait at least 5 hours afterwards.
- Choose a quiet location outdoors and away from people.
- Use dowsing to find 'neutral' ground. You should not locate or attune to your vivaxis on leys, grid lines or powerful earth energies.
- Make sure the ground is flat and free from electrical or magnetic disturbances, and is WiFi free.
- Avoid locating and channelling when planes are flying overhead.
- Use a compass to find the direction of your birthplace.
- Keep your mind relaxed.
- Your head should face the direction of your birthplace.
- Your clothing should not be touching your feet or the ground.
- Hold your head and spine ramrod-straight.
- Arms should be slightly away from the body.
- When turning to locate the wave channel the body must turn as a unit. Never twist or turn from the waist.

You need to do the following exercise alone. If other people are present their own energy fields may become disturbed.

Locating vivaxis energies

- Use either a compass to establish the direction of your birthplace and face it.
- Face your vivaxis and place your hands palm down firmly against the sides of your legs with feet tightly together.
- Your body may feel a slight forward pull in the direction of the vivaxis wave.
- Mark the position and put the rod and compass some distance away.
- Mark on the ground the opposite direction and the 90-degree side directions.
- You are now ready to channel the healing energies of your vivaxis.

Channelling vivaxis energies

The method that Frances devised for channelling the vivaxis wave is called the 'four by four' which will remove harmful foreign bodies and toxins from your energy field and allow the body to absorb healing energies in a two-way process. If you live in the northern hemisphere turn clockwise, and if you live in the southern hemisphere turn counter-clockwise whilst channelling your vivaxis.

- Make sure the directions are clearly marked on the ground.

- Place your hands palm down firmly against your legs which should be around 12 inches (30 centimetres) apart.

- Hold your head level and turn to your vivaxis.

- Close your eyes and breathe deeply through the nose.

- Slowly tilt your head downwards towards the chest and then

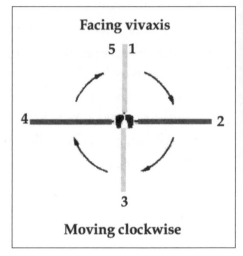

slowly back up to full extension of the neck backwards. This should take around 8 seconds. *Repeat this process for all the directions.*

- Open your eyes and turn 90 degrees to face position 2.

- With feet 12 inches (30 centimetres) apart and eyes closed, breathe deeply and tilt the head down and up. Remain like this for 8 seconds.

- Turn to position 3 – you are now standing with your back to your vivaxis and you may feel a slight pull backwards. Repeat the head-tilting procedure.

- Turn to position 4 – repeat the process of breathing and the head-tilting procedure.

- Finish by aligning a fifth time so that you are facing your vivaxis again.

- Move off the band and ground your hands on neutral ground to remove excess energy.

- Walk around for about 20 minutes to ground your energies and stay away from people while your body fluids are aligning to your vivaxis.

Many people claim that regular channelling once a week or month maintains a good connection with the Earth which promotes health and well-being, Benefits will include the body's ability to absorb minerals from the Earth and transfer them to your body whilst removing toxins and harmful bacteria or viruses.

Gaia's vivaxis

Earth is a part of the solar system and it revolves around the sun, taking one year to do so. No doubt Gaia senses and communicates with her lunar sister and feels her gravitational pull as well as the cosmic breath of the sun's solar wind upon her planetary body. Throughout the ages the physical and spiritual sun has been seen and depicted as a light force, or personified as the Heavenly Father, such as the Egyptian Ra. It is thought that the planets of the solar system, including the Earth, have their vivaxes rooted in the sun's physical-etheric body. Likewise, the sun revolves around the galactic centre and it may have its planetary vivaxis rooted therein. Younger galaxies may be connected to older galaxies as there is no separation. Everything in the universe is connected by an invisible magnetic cosmic cord of energy in two-way transmission, receiving and transmitting energy, the macrocosm united with the microcosm, all communicating with one another and bathing in the celestial tides of cosmic energy.

*There are many ways to connect to a sacred site
and to access its holy history.*

CHAPTER 13
Connecting to a sacred site

Sacred sites are spiritual teachers that can impart great wisdom. Constructed and programmed by an advanced civilization long gone who left behind their holy history and knowledge written in stone and earth. Temple complexes, stone circles and mounds act as portals to the Earth's Akashic Library, sacred wisdom, long lost technologies and spiritual evolution. Stone is predominantly silicon which, as we know, can store transmit and receive information, just like the silicon chips that revolutionized the computer age. Sacred sites with their earth patterns and mystical pathways are Earth Gates; locations were we can receive information and access planetary and celestial consciousness.

Gaia is sensitive to all life forms and her wisdom is immense. When we connect to the sensitive areas of her planetary body marked by sacred sites we become closer to Gaia and we can tap into her wisdom, knowledge, beauty and love. There are several ways in which we can open the Earth Gates to planetary consciousness. Earth Gates allow us to receive and impart universal information and unite us to Gaia mind-to-mind and heart-to-heart.

Connecting to Gaia and the Earth's Akashic Records

Attuning to a sacred site is a profound experience. One way to do this is to work with the site's earth energies, especially the geospiral, which has permanence, marks the heart of the site and will connect you to Gaia, the ancestors, the Earth's Akashic records or the site's holy history. Yin water is especially receptive and, like a tape recorder, it records and stores information within its spiral field. When we meditate above a geospiral we can access the water's memory field. Many people see, hear or simply sense images from the past or future, as time is circular rather than linear.

Standing stones rooted into the geospiral pattern likewise have an advanced memory code that ripples across time with the tidal pull of Earth's holy water.

Inspired by the author R. J Stewart I created a *geospiral mediation* which opens a wonderful Earth Gate and encourages a unique and mystical experience.

- Locate a geospiral and sit within its spiral coils.

- Imagine or sense that your entire body and aura is surrounded by a beautiful and resplendent golden light. You are radiant and protected within the splendour of this iridescent light *(See Psychic Protection Chapter 10).*

- In silent reverence, ask the sacred site for permission to contact Gaia, the Earth's Akashic Records or to receive/give healing. Set your intention.

- From your heart radiate love and gratitude. Honour the geospiral and Gaia.

- Visualize the geospiral as a circular closed door or hatchway in the ground before you. *If you are working in a group sit in a circle and collectively visualize the closed doorway at the centre.*

- Open the doorway or hatch with a clear affirmation of your intent and enter the earth to seek its spiritual light.

- See a beautiful descending spiral staircase gently curving towards the right (clockwise). The stair is cut into the natural rock and along the wall is a rail which you can hold as you begin your descent. The stairway leads to a sacred chamber, holy temple or a simple hollow within the earth. Sit within this temple space and feel the warmth of the earth around you as the healing light of the earth gently illuminates your temple space. Sit in silent contemplation, as at this stage various contacts are made or visions experienced. If you need advice, Gaia's wisdom or healing (for yourself or somebody else), simply ask and sense your request being received.

- When you feel ready ascend the spiral staircase and climb out through the circular doorway or hatch and always close it behind you.

- See the doorway fade into the earth so that it can no longer be seen.

- Give thanks and gratitude.

Working with magical springs

Contacting Gaia can also be made at holy wells or sacred springs. Paul Devereux noted that some holy wells naturally provoke a sleepy state that can change consciousness. At springheads, or old holy wells, we are in close proximity to a vast body of underground water which, as we have seen, are traditional portals for contacting Gaia.

Water is considered to be a feminine element and, at these watery sites we can easily sense the presence of the great Earth Goddess. Interestingly, most apparitions of the Blessed Virgin Mary have been at places associated with water. A famous example occurred in 1858. In a grotto, Bernadette Soubirous began pawing at the dirt and put the earth into her mouth until she retched. She did this until she found mud rather than dirt. The onlookers were totally perplexed until a spring erupted from the ground and the world famous Lourdes Water pored forth. Bernadette said that the Virgin had appeared to her and told her to drink the spring water and to wash in it.

In 1973 a London vicar and several other witnesses at St Mary's, Willesden, in North London, reported seeing a golden radiance which did not cast a shadow within the chapel. The church was founded in the 10th century and was a major centre for pilgrimage in medieval England after the Virgin had appeared and caused a spring to flow. It is the home to the ancient shrine of 'The Black Virgin of Willesdon', to which miraculous powers were ascribed. The famous Holy Water of Willesdon still flows underneath the church and is freely available to be taken away.

Another example of spring water and a vision of Mother Mary comes from La Saletter in France. In 1846 a young girl and boy saw a bright light near a stream. There they saw a holy lady in the light that spoke of local prophecies, all of which came to pass, and were confirmed to be true. Strangely, after the vision had ended, the holy lady dissolved from the head downwards leaving a brightness in the air and another stream formed from a spring which is now said to be healing.

Clearly, blind springs, holy springs and wells are special places where the Goddess manifests in a cultural guise that people can identify. Numerous sacred sites are associated with springs, streams or rivers and meditating close to sacred water is an uplifting experience. Here we are close to the Goddess and her all-healing energies.

The earthen circle of the Codford Ring lies close to Stonehenge.
The esoteric centre of the site has a high energy.

At night the elevated site connects you to the heavens above.

CHAPTER 14

Evidence

Most archaeologists and the scientific community dismiss the reality of leys and earth energies. Likewise, largely due to the lack of media coverage and evidence the majority of the population are totally unaware of the Earth's ever-present force. To the sceptic the existence of earth energy is purely anecdotal, despite the fact that energy lines have been documented since 2200 BC.

From 1954 to 1960 Guy Underwood conducted a large-scale study of the geodetic system of earth energies comprising individuals and large groups. Stonehenge was selected for several 'blind' studies; participants had no prior knowledge of where the geodetic lines or patterns flowed. Numerous testimonials endorsed Underwood's original findings as the energies dowsed by the participants matched Underwood's master survey. Likewise, during the 1990s my late father asked dowsing groups throughout the southwest of England to survey certain

Emperor Yu (2205-2197 BC) was famous for finding underground water, metals, hidden objects and more importantly for improving the Earth's fertility which can be increased or diminished at any site by the nature of the monument built there. He holds an unusual dowsing instrument.

locations for geodetic energies. The results corresponded and matched the original surveys. However, sceptics reject dowsing evidence as a non-scientific methodology. I realized that scientific confirmation of earth energies was necessary in order to prove their existence.

In search of the Dragon

Since the turn of the last century Master Dowsers have claimed that earth energies are intimately associated with sine wave motion and electromagnetic frequencies. If correct, electronic equipment should readily detect and record any emissions and so I asked two specialists to assist me. Rodney Hale is an expert in analyzing electromagnetic frequencies. He has worked alongside top British researchers such as Paul Devereux and John Steel who formed The Dragon Project Trust in the 1970s which was set up to investigate ancient sites with scientific instruments. Rodney was the project's chief electronics consultant. David Webb is a retired electrical engineer who has been researching the adverse effects of electromagnetic pollution for over 40 years. He offers expert advice to electromagnetic and chemical-sensitive people and his state-of-the-art equipment is used to ascertain the levels of electromagnetic pollution within their homes or workspaces.

The experiments we conducted were vastly different to the Dragon Project which investigated magnetic and radioactive radiation at certain sacred sites. Our investigations were selective and specialized as my primary focus was to examine earth energies within sacred sites. We wanted to analyse the location, flows and patterns of earth energy that were discovered by dowsing legends such as Guy Underwood, Dennis Wheatley, Hamish Miller and Paul Broadhurst. We wanted to see if the electronic equipment could pick up a signal where my dowsing rods detected a subterranean current. The tests were conducted using electromagnetic sensing equipment, wide-band radio receivers, a field mill (electrostatic), ion counter, spectrum analyzer, and volt metres. Most importantly, David Webb insisted that radio frequency meters were used which could instantly detect any man-made signal to show, categorically, that no such electrical fields were present. This is a must for all serious investigators, as it rules out man-made frequencies, and many are present creating an unseen electromagnetic smog (E-smog).

Back to the beginning - the Schumann Resonance

In the mid-1950s Dr. W. O. Schumann, a geophysicist, calculated that the Earth's ionosphere cavity produces a naturally occurring resonance, an electromagnetic frequency, called the 'Schumann Resonance', (SR) which was named after him. This natural pulse resonating around the planet beats at a frequency of 7.83-10 Hz. Earth's resonating 'heartbeat' is beyond our audible sense of hearing (infrasound). One of the first researchers to recognize the relationship of brainwave frequencies to the SR signals was Lewis B Hainsworth. Lewis noticed that Alpha brainwaves fall within the SR.

Brainwave frequencies and their Hertz signals

- Gamma waves fall between 25-60 Hz and relate to the processing of information from different areas of the brain involving learning, memory and integrating information.

- Beta waves fall between 12-25 Hz and dominate our normal waking state of consciousness. Beta is fast brainwave activity present when we are alert or even anxious, or when engaged in problem solving, decision making, information processing and general mental activity.

- Alpha waves fall between 8-13 Hz and are present during dreaming, relaxation and light meditation and when the eyes are closed. When the brain is in alpha mode we are naturally in resonance with the Earth's frequency.

- Theta waves fall between 4-7 Hz and naturally occur during sleep and deep meditation. In a theta state of consciousness the senses are withdrawn from the external world and one is focused on the inner world of the mindscape.

- Delta waves fall between 0-4 Hz and occur during deep, dreamless sleep.

Walking the Schumann Resonance (SR)

Chinese geomancers see subterranean energy as emitting a force which is either Sheng Chi, said to be benevolent, or Sha Chi which is a detrimental force of Nature. The landscape is seen in terms of opposing yin and yang energies which, as we read earlier, generates a vital force called ling. As part of our scientific experiments we decided to see if yin/yang earth currents emit an electromagnetic (sheng

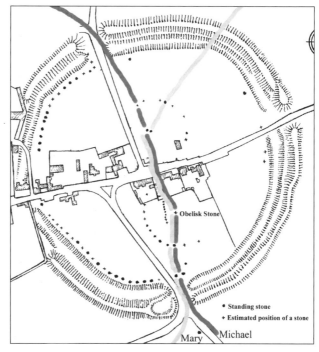

117

chi) frequency and if so analyze the signal. We selected the Mary yin current which flows through Avebury's stone circles like a mighty feminine river.

Close to the southeast entrance the Mary and Michael earth currents merge as one. Promoting balance and harmony the co-joined yin yang energies are said to have creative and transformative powers. Many people who have interacted with the Mary energy current say a sense of calm and peace engulfs them as they walk along the current's path.

Flowing towards the Avebury complex the Mary current is around 6 feet (1.82 metres) wide and it was here that Rodney Hale, Busty Taylor, and I took several measurements across its breadth. After careful analysis Rodney located three distinctive non-man-made signals which were measured in Hertz (Hz). These are shown in the following diagram as faint horizontal bands. At the current's centre (signal 1) a 7-10 Hz frequency was dominant which falls within the SR range. However, further away towards the outer edge the signal dramatically changed to a much higher frequency of 24-26 Hz (signal 3).

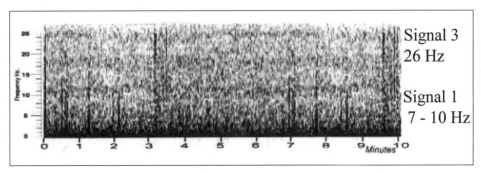

Healing frequency

Lower Hertz rates between 3-10 Hz produce a sense of well being, vitality and calmness, whereas higher frequencies such as gamma waves stimulate the mental faculties. Robert Beck researched the brainwave activity of healers from all different backgrounds and cultures including dowsers, shamans, wiccans, psychic and Christian healers and noted that during the 'healing moment' a 7.8-8 Hz brain wave activity was recorded on their EEG signature which lasted several seconds and synchronized with the Earth's pulse (SR). Remarkably, people receiving the healing did so at around 8 Hz which could be described as a 'healing frequency'. The Mary current's central frequency of 7-10 Hz falls within this range.

More than that, the Mary current's frequencies correspond to the full range of human brainwave activity ranging from gamma to alpha. Our research suggests that interacting with the Earth current's three primary frequency bands could encourage brainwave activity to synchronize with the Earth's emitted frequency. Interacting with the Mary current by walking slowly across it towards the near centre and following the current's central curvilinear path may encourage alpha brainwave activity, giving a sense of deep relaxation and inner peace. Certainly, this corresponds closely to anecdotal reports and experiences. If earth energies can influence brainwave activity walking slowly away from the centre to the outer edges should trigger mental activity – beta/gamma waves.

To the ancient Chinese the Mary yin energy was perceived as the White Tiger, the companion of the potent yang Green Dragon. Generating life-enhancing Sheng Chi the tiger was a potent symbol of feminine power and strength. Each age and culture interprets its surroundings using its own language patterns and metaphors. Today we apply science and technology to understand the dynamic living forces that the Earth emits which were accurately located and described by geomantic masters long gone.

25 Hz and levitation

Research into sound sine waves and levitation suggests that 25 Hz is the frequency of levitation. If correct, the natural earth energy frequency of 25 Hz which is present within the Mary current may have been manipulated by the megalithic builders who, in theory at least, could have created an oscillating magnetic energy field to raise the large stones along the 25 Hz flow.

Aquastatic energy

Guy Underwood discovered the aquastat energy flow which I have interpreted as an underground stream, or river, flowing predominantly with Earth's harmonic primary waters. But am I right? For years many geomancers, dowsers and dowsing societies have stated that all underground water is inharmonious to live above as it produces geopathic stress. Streams flow beneath the Earth from the geospiral along fissures, some of which are narrow and others can be exceptionally wide. David Webb located three narrow aquastat energy lines that flowed along Avebury's West Kennet Stone Avenue. If they produced geopathic stress this would be readily detected by the equipment. However, the aquastat streams gave a frequency of 10-12 Hz. This energy frequency confirms the harmonic aspect of the aquastat, as it falls within the Schumann Resonance range which is beneficial to health, unlike the high Hertz fields (geopathic stress) emitted by underground streams that flow predominantly with yang water.

Power points

Earlier we discussed earth springs and power points which my late father discovered at sacred sites and medieval churches in the UK and Europe. He insisted that they were healing energies. David Webb was intrigued by the idea that earth energy could rise out of the ground like a bubbling and babbling freshwater spring and conducted a series of scientific experiments to measure the air ions above selected power points. Ions are produced by cosmic and earth radiations and generally speaking negative ions are beneficial to health, whereas over-exposure to positive ions can be injurious. David Webb explains air ions in detail in Appendix 3.

The West Kennet Stone Avenue power point is marked by a standing stone. Directly in front of the megalith is a power point where energy pours out of the ground to roughly the height of the stone. My dowsing revealed that the power point is a small-contained area, and we wondered what the ion counter would detect. Groundbreaking results showed that the power point releases a vast quantity of negative ions whilst decreasing the amount of positive ions within its immediate vicinity. The ion counter recordings clearly show this. Over the power point the amount of positive ions recorded was 100 and the negative ion reading was 7,600. The control point which was only 11 feet (3.5 metres) away gave a dramatically different count of 1,093 positive ions and 5,040 negative ions. The difference in the positive ion count is staggering. The same test was conducted at various other power points and revealed a similar pattern, a radical depletion of positive ions whilst strangely increasing the negative ion count. The outpouring of negative ions gives a 'feel good factor' and a sense of well being and vitality.

> *At stone circles and other temple complexes power points are always located outside the monument. Avebury has two main power points; each one is sited along one of the stone avenues which were used as processional ways which led to the sanctity of the stone circles.*

One day I photographed the remains of the Beckhampton Stone Avenue which is shown below. Just after I had taken the photograph I suddenly felt the presence of the stones and got the distinct impression that they wanted me to return that evening to take a photograph over the nearby power point. And so I did. The photograph on the right is the evening shot of the power point which clearly shows its energetic power. My late father described a power point as a small fist-sized ball of energy that splays out like an umbrella above your head bathing you in energy and, as we now know, ionic energy. We have monitored

the ionic activity of the West Kennet Stone Avenue power point for several years and our results are consistent. We can say unequivocally that this type of earth energy is unique and showers us in unseen energy.

AC Readings at Avebury Henge

David Webb suggested that we record and analyze AC voltage readings over power points and earth energy locations within the Avebury complex. Our findings produced dramatic and consistent results and show that the electrical charge is radically different over a power point, producing a far lower reading than the nearby control zone, which was located 16 feet (5 metres) away. For instance, a major variation was recorded at the Sanctuary, which was once an integral part of the Avebury complex. At the centre of the stone circle where numerous energy lines converge the reading was 2,484 AC volts and away from the centre it immediately shot up to 11,779 volts. Similar readings occurred at the power point over the West Kennet Stone Avenue. Tentative results suggest that DC fields appear to do the reverse and are greater over the earth energy points. On going experiments will soon be able to confirm the enigmatic relationship with AC DC electrical fields within sacred sites and temple complexes.

The Cove - Avebury's healing zone

The Cove stones that stand within Avebury's northern inner circle were once a unique megalithic enclosure that consisted of three standing stones creating a horseshoe-shaped enclosure. Antiquarians stated that the stone circle contained around 27-30 stones and concentric with it was another stone circle composed of 12 stones. Visiting Avebury in 1663 Dr Charleton noted that the Cove had a fourth stone which he described as being 'triangular and of vast magnitude, lying flat on ye ground; but at first imposed on ye heads of ye other three in a manner of Architrave.'

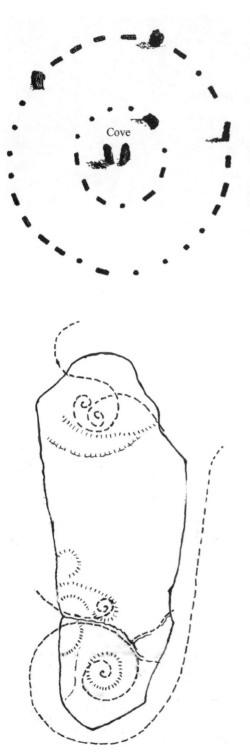

Recent archaeological investigations conclude that the triangular stone could not have been an overhead stone. The tops of the surviving Cove stones were examined in detail and it was evident that no capstone had ever been placed upon them. Archaeologists speculate that the stone was probably intended to be a floor stone and I suggest it designated an area where one could sit and soak up healing energies. The Cove was, and still is, a unique location set above a harmonic reversed circle that radically reduces the positive ion count and increases the negative ion count in a similar manner to a power point. No other location within the Avebury temple had a stone floor which was undoubtedly revered for its healing power. Dowsing suggests that the healing energy is released in a Fibonacci spiral.

Guy Underwood was one of the first dowsers to note that certain stones emit energy in a Fibonacci spiral. Standing against the stone, or lying upon it, allows direct contact to the energy flow which instantly interacts with an individual's energy field. Guy's illustration clearly shows this phenomenon. If you place the palm of your hand close to the energy spiral you will feel the energy release. I get people to experience this at the powerful bluestones of Stonehenge and also close to Chalice Well at Glastonbury.

Avebury's vast ditch may have contained water

Sacred surface water

Avebury henge is surrounded by a large ditch and bank which was set above a secondary halo that sanctified the site. Associated with a powerful blind spring at the near centre of the southern inner circle, the secondary halo serves not only to protect the site, but to consecrate any surface water it is sited above.

Avebury's ditch and bank is one of the most impressive earthworks in Britain. Remarkably, from the ditch over 90,000 cubic metres of chalk was removed, enough to build a pyramid with a 70 metre base and 46 metres high! The average volume of the seven pyramids of Egypt's Vth Dynasty is about the same as the contents of Avebury's massive ditch. Early twentieth century excavations showed that originally the ditch, close to the southern entrance, was 10-14 metres deep. In 1922, the archaeologist A.D. Passmore postulated that the ditch originally contained water creating a moat and stated: 'We can be sure that whenever there was water at the confluence, there was water in the huge moat.' However, his theory was quickly dismissed. In contrast, according to Maud Cunnington's archaeological expertise, the moat around Silbury Hill contained water all year round. So, why not Avebury's ditch?

Measurements of the water table taken from 1973-2002 by Thames Water support the moat hypothesis. Avebury Henge stands 160 metres at ground level. If the ditch was a uniform depth of 8-10 metres, it would have hit the water table. Today, even after much erosion and silting the ditch is still an impressive

5 metres deep. The graph clearly shows water at 150 metres. This would give an estimated water depth of 3-4 metres. Although, during especially hot or dry summers, such as 1976, 1992 and 1997-8 the water table dropped significantly; however, overall it remains fairly consistent.

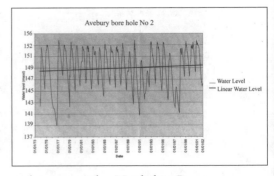

Interestingly, in the oldest European language, the Neolithic Basque tongue, *Urberri* means 'New Water'. True to the nature of mythical reality, the henge water was new not only in 2600 BCE but every spring filling the moat afresh as the water table reached saturation.

A large 7-coiled geospiral dictated the location of the Rollright Ring. Changing rotational direction synchronizing with the moon's six-day lunar phases, the geospiral perpetually generates vortex energy.

To understand Rollright's energy David Webb and I decided to conduct several measurements within and outside the stone circle using an ion counter. The ion counts were stable outside the stone circle, measuring 270 positive ions and 280 negative ions, and these were used for the control reading. At the centre of the geospiral the readings changed dramatically. The positive ion count was 80 – that is a staggering reduction of 190, and the negative ion count was 9,230 making a significant change of 8,950 ions. The circle of stones influences the reading as the energy spins around the circle and leaves at what is called the 'exit gate' which produced similar readings. The linear beam passes laser-like across the countryside and targets a solitary standing stone known as 'The Hawk Stone',

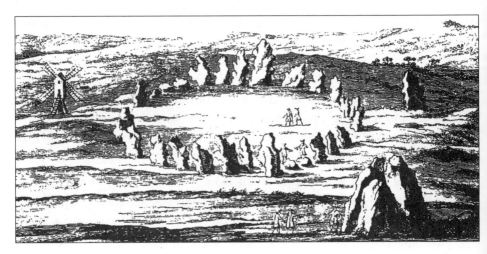

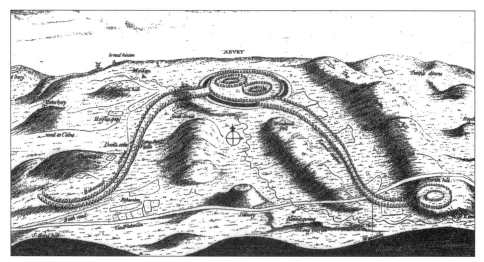

The Beckhampton Avenue was set by an energy current called the Beckhampton Serpent and, likewise, the West Kennet Stone Avenue was aligned upon the Michael earth energy current

six miles (9.65 kilometres) to the south on the appropriately named Spelsbury Down. Enhanced by the circular shape the geospiral energy is intensified and generates a perpetual supply of free electromagnetic energy.

Genesis leys and Knoll Down

Knoll Down near Avebury is magical! Tall beech trees guard the Neolithic earthworks; their long branches sway and the leaves rustle in the wind reminding us why the Druids chose groves to worship in. Full of atmosphere and energy, Knoll Down is a must for the earth mystery enthusiast.

Hamish Miller and my late father thought that the earthworks on Knoll Down were the location of William Stukeley's serpent tail – where the Beckhampton Stone Avenue terminated (or began). However, Stukeley insisted the avenue ended near the Bronze Age barrows at Fox Covert which is situated *below* Knoll Down. He actually saw and recorded the path of the avenue.

Nonetheless, local dowser Brian Ashley discovered an energy line which ran from the west of Avebury Henge along the High Street, past the church and out into the fields of Manor Farm. Brian called this energy line the *Beckhampton Serpent* and it continues its course between the Longstones and on through the nearby Longstones long barrow. The energy line emerges from two ram-horn spirals (as previously described in the section on Genesis leys); however, some 15 years ago we discovered that there are several ram-horn spirals associated with the Beckhampton serpent, although the two spirals that Brian originally discovered are the largest and these are located towards the western end of the earthworks.

The Beckhampton Avenue was set by an energy current called the Beckhampton Serpent and, likewise, the West Kennet Stone Avenue was aligned upon the Michael earth energy current.

David Webb and I conducted several experiments over the ram-horn emergence spirals that my late father discovered. Vortex-like, these erupting energy points produced some startling readings. The frequency metre recorded cyclic frequencies of 10 Hz with a 6-second gap, rising to 20 Hz, another gap rising to 40 Hz, followed by another gap, and then 60 Hz. David Webb was astonished as he had never recorded anything like this before; something very unusual was occurring. The control readings were standard for the area, moreover unchanging. The 10, 20, 40, 60 Hz cyclic frequency may be due to the curvature of the ram-horn. Standing above the vortex can be energizing but we suggest for a short period of 3 minutes only as the energy is very powerful. Male vortex energy can be especially energizing and anecdotal evidence suggests it can connect you to your spiritual purpose. The female vortex appears to expand your creativity or intuition.

Capturing earth energy

It was mentioned earlier that Harry Oldfield claims to have made a camera filter which can photograph earth energy. If correct, and the filter is not just capturing light, then the end result is outstanding. Mervin, one of Oldfield's former colleagues, joined me at Uffington in Oxfordshire to take a series of photographs using the filter. I asked him to photograph the male and female vortices on the summit of Dragon Hill, as here the emerging energy is particularly strong. The energy lines join as one forming a powerful hermaphrodite Genesis ley that courses across the ceremonial landscape and terminates within a Neolithic burial chamber.

We gained incredible insight into the nature of Genesis energy and alongside the Hertz frequency recordings at Knoll Down confirmed this type of earth energy exists, and was not a figment of my late father's imagination. Many dowsers, as well as sceptics, scoffed at the idea of Genesis energy!

According to Oldfield's filter earth energy rises out of the Earth in horizontal bands of rainbow-coloured light, with red being closest to the ground and the other colours rising vertically. Surprisingly, the emerging and descending Genesis energy appears to follow a specific colour sequence. Emerging Genesis earth energy rises out of the ground in rainbow colour succession with red emerging first through to violet. However, descending Genesis energy does the reverse; the higher chakra colours of violet are the first to descend into the ground and red is the last colour to re-enter.

Thanks to David Webb and Rodney Hale the Earth's invisible energy has been scientifically measured. Earth energies can no longer be dismissed as nonsense as their emissions can be analysed for voltage, Hertz frequency, ionic or electromagnetic anomalies. Certainly, dowsing, alongside our scientific enquiries, has proven beyond all reasonable doubt that *something* strange happens over earth energies which influences the Hertz frequency, air ions and electrical charge within temple space.

*Our scientific experiments have verified earth energies.
However, the real evidence is how earth energies make us feel.*

*I showed Canadian rock band The Saints of British Rock
many sacred sites and they felt the power in the land.*

CHAPTER 15
Back to the future

Worldwide earth energies were skilfully integrated into the foundation plans of sacred sites. As we have seen, the first design canon was to locate the geospiral with its three-fold energy pattern which releases invisible harmonic power and silently imbues the site with healing, uplifting and protective energy. Once the earth energy was located sacred geometry and celestial alignments were incorporated which amplified the monument's terrestrial and cosmic power. Leys distributed energy across the landscape in a network that is still partially active and its invisible flow can be felt by those who are sensitive.

But where did this knowledge originate? Certainly, geomancy and the art of sacred site placement in Europe can be traced to c12000-10000 BC as many Mesolithic sites and settlements, such as Göbekli Tepe and Karahan Tepe in Turkey and Starr Carr close to the river Hartford in Yorkshire, testify. Did the later Neolithic people who constructed the megalithic wonders of the ancient world inherit the advanced technical knowledge from their ancestors and, if so, who were they?

Atlantis

Plato wrote of Atlantis around 355 BC and his books *Critias* and *Timaeus* speak of the splendours of a long-lost civilization in the Atlantic Ocean. One of his friends, Critias, said that Atlantis is 'derived from ancient tradition'. Not everyone agreed. Aristotle fervently disagreed

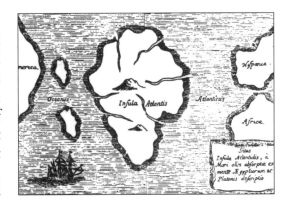

and believed that Plato had made Atlantis up and this doubt has persisted ever since. Nevertheless, Plato goes out of his way to report exactly where the original Atlantis tale came from. Solon, a famous Greek elder, had been given the story by an Egyptian priest, Sais, and told what he knew to an equally renowned Greek, Critias, whose grandson was a friend of Socrates and narrated the story in Plato's books. All of these people were considered trustworthy and honourable. Plato himself affirmed: 'The fact that it is not an invented fable but a genuine history is all-important.' According to these ancient sources Atlantis was situated beyond the Pillars of Hercules – the Straits of Gibraltar – amid the Atlantic Ocean.

Plato describes the Atlantean metropolis as being circular. He comments: *'At the centre of the island, near the sea, was a plain, said to be the most beautiful and fertile of all plains and near the middle of this plain about 50 strades inland a hill of no great size. There were two rings of islands, three of seas, like cartwheels with the island at their centre...In the centre a shrine sacred to Poseidon and Cleito surrounded by a golden wall.'*

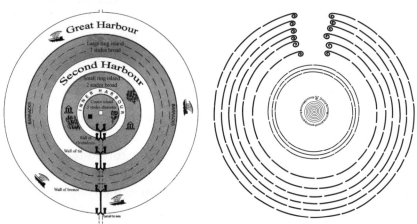

Harmonic placement

Did the Atlantean architects integrate the Earth's powerful geometries into the foundation plans of their great city? According to Plato's accounts of the city and its functions geodetic engineering seems likely.

Plato describes the central hill in the city as having two springs, one hot and one cold, which surfaced from underground streams. He states that the city's water was 'remarkable quality and excellence'. This suggests no ordinary aquifer and indicates sacred yin water. Moreover, Plato describes the water as 'pure water' which fed buildings and the surrounding landscape, and outflows led to

Poseidon's sacred grove and temple. Water was also channelled into the outer ring by ingenious aqueducts and a bridge so that each island was encircled by the Earth's healing waters. The water also irrigated a vast plain which was said to be 230 x 340 miles (370 x 547 kilometres). Plato remarked on the island's lush fertility 'whatever fragrant things that are now on the Earth...all these that sacred island brought forth fair and wondrous and in infinite abundance.' Additional confirmation that the springs were yin water is confirmed by the circular shape of Atlantis. As we have seen, stone circles, earthen mounds and later Templar churches were all circular dictated by the primary and secondary halo patterns associated with the geospiral. The Atlantean civilization, through its geomancers, was one of the first to incorporate earth energies into city planning.

Encoding the Earth's diameter

The city was said to be 15 miles in diameter and I intuitively felt this number would prove significant and represent the Earth in some way. I converted miles to feet and made an extraordinary discovery – 15 miles equals 79,200 feet exactly. If this number is divided by 10 it equals 7,920 which, according to the late John Michell, 'is the average diameter of the Earth as measured in feet'. Remarkably, the diameter of the Atlantean city mathematically represented the Earth's diameter.

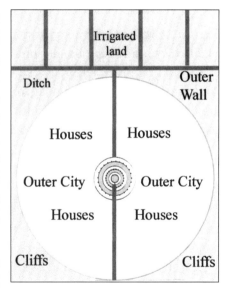

After the great deluge engulfed the mighty continent, which was recorded by numerous cultures across the globe, remnants of their sophisticated geomantic practices survived. Distant lands were colonized, the knowledge of the Earth's energetic system was distributed and a monumental prehistoric building programme began. Epicentres were created which collected and distributed the Earth's power, such as pyramids, stone circles and other holy constructs, all of which stand as silent witnesses to a collective cultural practice adopted worldwide, as sacred sites from Siberia to Easter Island incorporate identical geodetic design canons born of Atlantis.

Utilizing Atlantean knowledge

Ancient wisdom can be applied to a modern generation. By adopting old geomantic practices we can spiritualize our homes and workspaces. Divining the hidden geodetic signature of our home or locality allows us to understand its energy and reveals why people become ill in certain houses or why certain businesses flourish. Location is all-important. Future building projects could implement geomantic awareness and create constructs which will benefit and serve humanity whilst living in harmony with Gaia's energies. A building project could begin by analysing the land's harmonic signature and architectural design could be guided by its energetic quality. Imagine for one moment a future hospital. First, the 3-fold harmonic pattern - the geospiral, primary and secondary haloes could be located. Areas that required stimulating energies such as physiotherapy and similar departments could benefit from the faster flowing energies or sections of the primary halo. In Atlantean times the ring island was aligned upon a primary halo which was suitably used to exercise horses and for athletic games and physical exercises.

Returning to our imaginary hospital, the placement of healing areas could be planned by branch spirals, geospirals and aquastat crossing points and the entire area could be protected by a secondary halo. The horseshoe or circular shape could transform the rectangular architectural framework of the old materialistic era returning us to esoteric Atlantean design. Likewise, other properties such as schools, offices and our homes could benefit from geodetic engineering whilst avoiding geopathic stress zones.

Geopathic stress

Medical studies have shown that living upon sections of the Hartmann, Curry, or Benker grids, can be injurious to health as the lines produce geopathic stress zones as do negative leys and underground yang water. (The Hartmann and Curry grid systems were discussed in *The Essential Dowsing Guide*.)

During 1988 to 1995 a German medical team led by Andreas Kopschina conducted a seven-year study of geopathic stress which involved 8,200 patients; they measured the ability of patients to recover from chronic illness regardless of the type of conventional or holistic therapy they received. Part of the study consisted of exposing 34% of patients to significant levels of geopathic stress. The study showed categorically that when a person was taken away from the geopathic stress zone their capacity to heal was greatly improved. Dr Ulrike Banis, MD, ND, noted that at least 30% of all chronic medical conditions are derived from geopathic stress. Dr. Banis concluded that patients would be, on average, 30% healthier if they managed to find geopathic-stress-free sleeping zones.

The Benker Grid

The Benker grid discovered by Anton Benker is highly toxic and it runs north-south and east-west. The injurious lines are approximately 8-11 inches (21-30 centimetres) wide and form a grid 32 feet (10 metres) wide. Like the other grids previously discussed in *The Essential Dowsing Guide* the lines are polarised, and these are shown opposite.

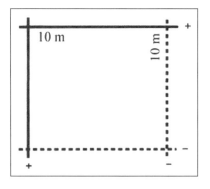

You can locate the Benker grid lines by simply 'tuning in' to them. Visualize the lines as walls of silver light and use information dowsing to locate them. Analyse your findings – the width of the grid lines and, if possible, their distance apart, so that you know with certainty that you dowsed a toxic Benker grid line.

Evidence

Research has shown that positive ions emanate from the grid lines which have a detrimental effect as they lower oxygen levels in the rooms of our homes to uncomfortable levels. Over prolonged time periods lower oxygen levels can potentially lead to unhealthy cell growth. The adverse crossing points and double lines of the Hartmann, Curry and Benker lines produce geopathic stress zones as they emit harmful energy radiations, produce changes in the Earth's magnetic field and some show an increase in radioactivity (gamma rays). Long-term exposure to these energies, such as sleeping over them, can be inimical to health. Check the bed positions of the household and harmonize their placement; if the bed is located upon a grid line simply move it away from the line or crossing point. This practice should be mandatory in all hospitals and care homes.

Symptoms of geopathic stress zones

- Aversion to going to bed and being unable to sleep for hours.
- Restless sleep.
- Avoiding certain points in the bed.
- Sleepwalking.
- Feeling cold in bed, chattering teeth and night sweats.
- Waking fatigued and apathetic.

- Depression, nervousness, despondency, crying after wakening.
- Cramps and heart palpitations.
- Poor physical performance.
- Reduced classroom performance if students sit and work upon the grid lines.
- Research has also shown that waking up between 2am and 3am often coincides with sleeping over a geopathic stress zone as geopathic stress reaches a maximum at this time of the night.

Earth's energy lines and patterns silently show us beneficial and injurious locations and these were recognized by our ancestors who lived in harmony with the Earth. However, in recent times when our world became industrialized and the consumer age was born many people became disconnected from the earth. Synthetic materials replaced Gaia's natural materials and factories replaced farms. In times gone by we allowed agricultural land time to rest, to stay fallow and regenerate, as the old-style farmer knew that the land would become exhausted. Today chemicals act as aggressive stimulants forcing the earth to stay awake when really she wants to sleep and return to her dreamtime. Our greed for material goods has ignored the well-being of Gaia. The tides are turning. A growing number of people are reconnecting to power places which are activating deep soul memories. Places like Stonehenge and the pyramids are attracting more and more pilgrims and many people change their lives after visiting such places.

These sacred locations once created a global energetic network as magnetic dragon energy was directed from the high mountains and hills to flow along the leys and stone avenues and coil around the stone monuments. The hidden veins coursing deep within the land were manipulated by the ancient sages who created a science of spiritual engineering whose ruins are still visible in every corner of the globe.

For the modern-day pilgrim visiting a power place is a spiritual experience. The song of the land is amplified at a sacred site and its holy energies silently encourage us to reconnect and commune with the earth. Voices, visions and images can often be heard and seen which activate a spiritual (re)awakening which can raise consciousness. Collectively many of us are sensing the need to return to our Mother's arms. We are reconnecting to the earth and our hunger for consumerism is being replaced by a thirst for sacred knowledge. Power places stir us to remember what was and what will be again, gently calling us to walk the path that permits equality, justice and fairness for all of

Gaia's children, no matter what colour, race or creed. Secrets of the land that were only known by the selected few are now being understood by the many. No longer concealed by secret societies, or selective Mystery Schools, esoteric knowledge is being shared. Admittedly many secrets are still hidden in places like the Vatican vaults which are kept under lock and key; however, open them with your heart mind as the Piscean Age of concealment is over.

Over the years I have shown many people such as engineers, nuclear physicists and nursing staff how to live in harmony with the earth and I have also reconnected Catholic clerks to recognise the power of the land and to honour the Goddess principle. Make no mistake, the tides are turning. Architects have asked my opinion regarding creating new living spaces that are alive with the Earth Force. You too can honour the Old Ways and heart to heart and hand in hand we can change the world in which we live and together we will create Heaven on Earth.

CHAPTER 16
Experience the Earth Force

B elow are a number of power places where you can experience and divine specific earth energy patterns that are particularly strong and peculiar to the area.

The Uffington White Horse complex

Many diverse leys and earth energies can be experienced in the legendary landscape of Uffington which is steeped in myths and Arthurian tales.

Dragon Hill

According to the 17th century antiquarian John Aubrey Dragon Hill is the tumulus of Uther Pendragon, King Arthur's father. 'That Uther Pendragon fought against the Saxons is certayne: perhaps was here slayne, from whence Dragon Hill may take its denomination.' The hill's summit is sculptured flat and was once used for ceremonial activity long before King Arthur. One of the most powerful places to experience a Genesis line is on Dragon

Hill. On the hill's summit dowse for a Genesis ley which emerges from two 'ram-horn spirals', the yin and yang vortices are powerful and cause the rod to spin wildly *(See Chapter 3)*. The line flows to Wayland's Smithy where it enters a burial chamber.

The Uffington White Horse

- Check the outline of the horse to see if it is encased by living aquastat parallels symbolically bringing the figure to life.

- Dowse the head area and locate the 'dragon horns' – the remanence of its once more dragon-like appearance as recorded by Guy Underwood in the 1950s.

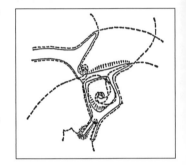

Uffington Castle

Uffington Castle is classified as an Iron Age hill fort but it certainly was not built to be defensive and so is more likely to have been a Druidic ceremonial centre. Gary Biltcliffe and Caroline Hoare discovered that the Elen dragon current coursed through the causeway entrances. Belinus, the male dragon current, enters through the ramparts and crosses Elen at the near centre.

Wayland's Smithy long barrow

- The Genesis line that emerged from Dragon Hill courses along the barrow's axis.

- Locate the descending section of the line as previously described in Chapter 3. Place the palm of your hand

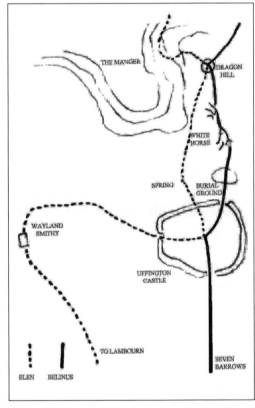

about 10 inches (25 centimetres) above this area. Sensitive people feel a magnetic pull towards the Earth.

The Ridgeway

Nearby is an ancient Mesolithic trackway called the Ridgeway which was used by prehistoric people. It crosses an old lane about a quarter of a mile before Wayland's Smithy long barrow. Crossroads were sacred to the great Goddess Hecate and also to the god Hermes. In medieval times alleged vampires were never staked, they were buried at a crossroads so that upon their ghoulish awakening they would not know which way to turn and thus be forever trapped. Ancient crossroads have power. Track lines converge and cross one another at a crossroads creating an energetic portal.

One day I met an old lady at this crossroads and she was tapping the ground rhythmically. I thought she had lost or dropped something and offered my assistance. I asked her what she was doing and she replied: 'Calling upon the Old One.' I thought I felt the ground shudder – or was it my imagination? Either way I felt uncomfortable and so hurried off towards the car park. I sat down near the car and began to look through my bag and a cough drew my attention to look up. The old lady was standing a few metres in front of me, yet she had not overtaken me along the narrow track. She smiled at me and walked off! Which way she walked I will never know!

- Locate the track line that once set the size of the old Neolithic Ridgeway and lane.

- Tune into one of the lines and track it to the centre of the crossroads.

- Now hold the rod a few inches from the ground. Slowly raise it; when it picks up on the powerful energy funnel it will either spin or judder.

Merlin's Mount, Marlborough College, Wiltshire

Tucked in the grounds of the prestigious Marlborough College is Merlin's Mount, a Neolithic man-made wonder that is connected in some way to the Avebury complex. It is exactly half the height of its contemporary big sister, Silbury Hill, which is sited just a few miles away. Marlborough's Royal Castle used to stand on the summit and a spring once fed a moat at the foot of the mount mirroring Silbury's watery image. On the southern side of the hill is a grotto ornamented with hundreds of seashells called Lady Hertford's Grotto. During excavations red deer antlers were found some 2-3 feet (0.60-0.91 metres) within the mound.

A possible derivation of the name Marlborough from Saxon is Moerla-Beorh 'Merlin's Barrow or burial place'. Supporting this theory the motto on the Borough Arms reads 'Ubi nunc sapientis ossa Merlini' *where now are the bones of the wise Merlin.*

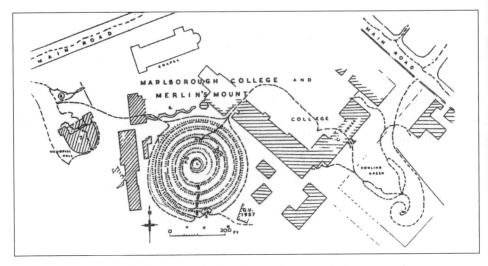

- Locate a 7-coiled geospiral which sets the size of the mound.

- A grid pattern of Earth energy can be located in the northern sector, close to the rose garden which was shown to my father by a senior lecturer who was visiting the college. He said: *the real power [of the mound] lies in the grid to the north of the mound.* That it does!

The Sanctuary. Avebury. Colour line dowsing

In the 18th century William Stukeley depicted the Avebury Henge complex as a mighty serpent. The serpent's head was represented by a small stone circle called the Sanctuary on Overton Hill; its neck was the West Kennet Stone Avenue, Avebury's stone circles the body and its tail was the Beckhampton Avenue, although, it must be said, there were four entrances each of which was served by a megalithic avenue. The stone circle that once crowned Overton Hill was a power place but it was destroyed during the stone-smashing holocaust that took place around the 1720s.

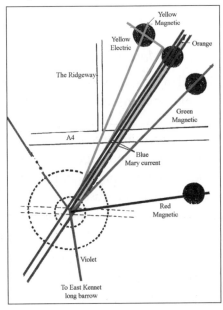

Nearly all the colours of the earth spectrum are found at the Sanctuary making it an ideal location to experience the rainbow colours within the land and explore the art of colour dowsing.

- Locate the colour lines and interpret their frequency. Interacting with electric lines can be counteracted by spending 10 minutes or so upon a magnetic line or the Mary or Michael dragon currents.

- Use your hands to compare the red magnetic line, which runs close to the surface, to the higher frequency of the spiritual violet line. Can you sense or feel a difference?

Carnac, France

Carnac is an immense megalithic complex located in Brittany, France. Eleven stone rows course across the landscape for around four miles (6.43 kilometres) containing some 1,099 standing stones. Decades ago French water diviners asserted that the stone rows were sited above eleven underground streams. Map dowsing revealed that several of the streams are aquastats and some are holy lines. The yang water/stream bands that emit geopathic stress are converted to harmonic energy by the aquastatic streams and their parallels. Today Carnac is seen from a viewing platform, and so interacting with its sea of aquastat energy system is not permitted. Below is a drawing of a gigantic menhir of Kerloaz 1861.

Le Grand Menhir Brisé Around 4500 BC the largest standing stone in Europe was erected called *Le Grand Menhir Brisé*. Standing over 65 feet (20 metres) high it is estimated to have weighed about 355 tons. Originally it was the largest standing stone of a 19-stone row alignment. Remarkably it may have stood intact for more than 6,000 years until it fell in the 18th century. The late John Michell records an Admiralty

An impression of the design of the original structure.
The stones once stood in a line decreasing in height from Le Grande Menhir Brisé.

report of 1659 on a local shipwreck, which noted that: 'la Grande pierre de Locmariaker was visible from the scene of the wreck' and a drawing by Robien from 1725 shows the stone fallen, which places the time of the fall sometime between 1659 and 1725. It was thought that an earthquake in 1722 was to blame and computer modelling of the toppled stone supports this hypothesis. Today the fallen stone lies in four pieces and was hand 'mauled' into its shape, and an axe-plough figure was once fully visible on the middle fragment.

Lunar alignments

The original construction of the 19-stone row alignment was one of Europe's greatest megalithic achievements. Prof. Alexander Thom noted that Le Grand Menhir Brisé served as a lunar marker to accurately calculate the 18.61-year lunar cycle by observing the largest stone from positions in the surrounding countryside. He predicted, and later found, the exact sighting locations that acted as ancient markers and he concluded that Le Grand Menhir Brisé was a huge foresight marker for the moon's rising and setting extremes.

Experience remanence dowsing

One of the most intriguing aspects about objects is that when they are moved they leave behind a three-dimensional etheric ghost of their past presence and this can be readily detected with a single rod in 'search'. Standing stones that have been toppled or completely removed leave behind their 'remanence' trace, that is to say their original width and height. With a single rod in 'search' make a dowsing pass, from any direction, towards the original location of Le Grand Menhir Brisé using your accuracy reference. As the reference coincides with the remanence of the outer skin of where the stone once stood the rod will zap into 'found'. It's as if you have encountered the stone itself, so powerful is the reaction.

Fort Ancient and Moon City. Warren County, Ohio

Fort Ancient is the largest prehistoric enclosure in the USA, which was constructed around 100 BC-500 AD by the Hopewell culture.

Fort Ancient consists of a series of meandering earthen banks which extend for more than three and half miles (5.6 kilometres) around a high bluff along the Little Miami River in Warren County, Ohio. The word 'fort' is misleading as this was not a defensive enclosure; the ditches were located inside the wall-like banks with more than 60 gates or breaks within the earthwork. Fort Ancient shares striking similarities with British henges and older Neolithic causewayed enclosures such as Windmill Hill near Avebury which is over five and a half thousand years old.

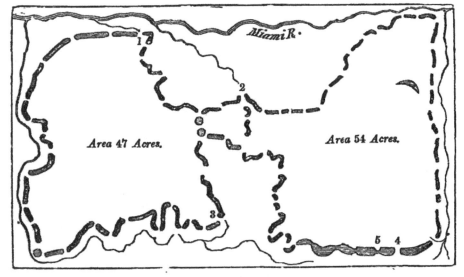

FORT ANCIENT.

143

Close to Stonehenge lies the Durrington Walls enclosure, once a bustling town that housed the people that built Stonehenge. After Stonehenge was completed, around 2500 BC, it became a 'super henge' enclosing 42 acres, a similar size to one of Fort Ancient's enclosures. The ditches of both monuments were 18 feet (5.48 metres) deep.

Ingenious design and Moon City

According to a 19th century antiquarian who travelled alongside a Native American called Dee-Coo-Dah, the earthen walls of Fort Ancient ranged from 8 to 18 feet (2.43-5.48 metres) high. However, tradition states that in places the earthen walls were gigantic and over 30 feet (9.14 metres) high that 'towered above the tops of the highest trees.' The clay-like soil used to construct the banks resisted saturation and its rainproof oily texture ensured preservation. Accounts of its water-resistant properties were observed in the spring of 1858. Rainfall stayed on the surface until the warmer weather caused evaporation and annual maintenance of the banks was made trouble-free as the oily texture made removal of decomposed material easy.

Moon City

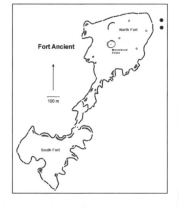

Remarkably, the interior of around 100 acres was sculptured flat and one enclosure contained a large crescent moon shaped earthwork. This enclosure was called 'Moon City' and Dee-Coo-Dah spoke of his culture's customs that saw the moon as the divine abode of the departed spirits of females. The earlier traditions of the original inhabitants are lost and long gone, although Dee-Coo-Dah recalled that Fort Ancient was constructed by a 'long line of noble kings or rulers'. Throughout the ancient world the moon was associated with the feminine principle, intuitive powers, and the moon mound may well have been used for divination, prophecy and healing. Also sited within the boundaries of the so-called north fort is an earthen feature called the 'Moorehead Circle' which resembles the symbol of the sun – a circle with a central dot. Whether or not this was intended to be a solar motif is unknown; however, temple complexes such as Avebury Henge have areas that were dedicated to the sun and moon as were monuments in Mexico.

America in Earth

This impressive earthwork is said to be a symbolic representation of North and South America and a possible reference to the uniting of the two lands and its peoples.

Dowsing the site

Fort Ancient offers beautiful vistas along a hiking trail as well as the remains of the marvellous ancient earthworks. Picnic areas can be found along the trail.

- Check the remaining mounds and see if a portion of them are set by aquastats.
- Check how far the aquastat parallels extend creating a healing field.
- Dowse for a genesis ley.
- Dowse for track lines.
- Dowse for holy lines.
- According to antiquarian sources sections 1, 2 and 3, which are shown in the first illustration, relate to water; confirm if this correct. What type of water was it – predominantly yin or yang?

Newark – the greatest earthworks in the world. Newark, Ohio

If the archaeological dating sequence is correct Newark was constructed by the Hopewell civilization between 100 BC-500 AD. It is one of the wonders of the prehistoric world. Two centuries ago Dee-Coo-Dah said that his native people called it the *Prophet's Metropolis*, and today it attracts thousands of visitors each year. Mile after mile of embankments, avenues, lodge-sites and mounds make this site the largest earthen temple complex in the world, spanning some 3,000 acres. The main features are the Great Circle Earthworks which are nearly 1,200 feet (365.76 metres) in diameter, the Octagon Earthworks enclosing 50 acres which is linked by parallel walls to a smaller circle enclosing 20 acres, and the Wright Earthworks, a large, nearly perfect square enclosure. Much of the site has been destroyed but the Great Circle, a 50-foot-long (15.24 metres) segment of the Newark Square, and various other earthworks have survived the passage of time.

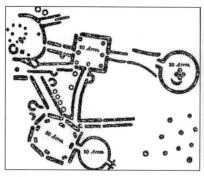 

Ohio Historical Society's archaeologist Bradley Lepper thinks that the Hopewell Culture built these vast ceremonial spaces as people from hundreds, if not thousands, of miles away came to Newark making it an epicentre of national importance. Impressive avenues up to 6,000 feet (1828.8 metres) long connected the various enclosures, but, as we shall soon see, extended avenues connected sacred site to sacred site across Ohio's ceremonial landscape.

Mysteries structure and Eagle Mound According to antiquarian reports the gigantic walls of the great circular enclosure towered up to 16 feet (4.87 metres) high and were 50 feet (15.24 metres) thick at the base with an inner ditch that was 13 feet (3.96 metres) in depth. Centrally located within the Great Circle is Eagle Mound which was a group of connected mounds that may have been an effigy of a bird in flight. In 1928 Emerson Greenman excavated the mound for the Ohio State Museum. Several postholes were discovered indicating a large structure 100 feet (30.48 metres) long by 23 feet (7 metres) wide which once stood prior to the mound. At the centre was a clay basin 10 feet (3.04 metres) long by 5 feet (1.52 metres) wide and about 5 inches (12.7 centimetres) in depth, built deep into the centre of the floor. Although no bones or ashes were found in the basin archaeologists assumed it was used for funereal rites. Lacking supportive evidence this assumption is just a wild guess. Until we look at sacred sites as places for the living rather than for the dead we will never fully understand their purpose.

Certainly, the structure and its mysterious basin designated a special place, possibly where shamans or spiritual leaders conducted ceremonies. Or was it once used to harness some form of earth or ley energy by prehistoric engineers? When the shamanic or engineering activities were completed the wooden structure was removed and a mound was built over the remains of the place. Within Stonehenge there was a similar feature. A pit was dug close to the greater trilithon that was 39 feet (11.80 metres) long, 16 feet (4.87 metres) wide, and 7 feet (2.13 metres) deep which baffles archaeologists. Why it was built remains one of the unanswered mysteries of Stonehenge and also of Newark.

Octagon Earthworks

The illustration of the Great Circle shows a crescent-moon-shaped mound which was around 200 feet (60.96 metres) long. The moon's cycle featured prominently at Newark and was ingeniously incorporated into the earthworks. For many years the large loaf-shaped mound located along the southeastern edge of the Octagon Earthworks has been called the 'observatory' simply because it provided a convenient observation platform for visitors to view the earthworks. The name proved to be highly appropriate as professors from Earlham College, Indiana, Ray Hively and Robert Horn found the Octagon Earthworks served as an ancient observatory. If you stand on Observatory Mound and look straight down the set of parallel walls that connect the circle with the Octagon you are looking at the point on the horizon where the moon rises at its most northerly position. This alignment requires astronomical precision as it only happens once every 18.61 years. Originally the loaf-shaped mound's outer surface was faced with limestone slabs making it appear white which, no doubt, poetically reflected the moon's silvery light.

Ley alignments

According to Brad Lepper, the parallel walls that extended in a straight line from the Octagon enclosure may have connected the site to another Hopewell enclosure near Chillicothe which is some 60 miles (96.5 kilometres) away. Brad calls this the Great Hopewell Road which may have been a route of pilgrimage which I suspect is aligned upon a vast ley that united two of the largest centres of the Hopewell world and was similar to the straight roads built by the Maya culture in Mesoamerica called *sacbeob*, or white roads. One antiquarian source states that 'extensive ranges of mounds, extending sometimes in direct and continuous lines for several hundreds of miles [Earthen] effigies which are always found at points where the principal lines intersect each other, or are joined by lines diverging laterally, as seen in Iowa, Wisconsin, and Circleville, in Ohio'. Evidently an earthen effigy marked the crossing point of major leys.

Visiting the site

Great Circle, Octagon Earthworks and Wright Earthworks are open all year during daylight hours. The Octagon Earthworks is also the site of the Moundbuilders Country Club, but there is a viewing platform near the parking area. The golf course halts play four times a year, allowing visitors to see the earthworks up close.

Remanence dowsing the earthworks

At Newark you can experience the powerful remanence of the henge bank's width. With a single rod in 'search' make a dowsing pass, from any direction, towards the ground marker, using your accuracy reference. As the reference coincides with the remanence of the outer skin of the missing bank the rod will zap into 'found'. Continue tuning into the bank's width and you will get another reaction when the rod has detected the bank, revealing its former gigantic width.

- Dowse sections of the Ohio Trail to ascertain if it is aligned on a major ley.

- If so, check the ley for associated yin and yang dragon currents, which my map dowsing indicates. To date no ley and its accompanying yin yang currents have been located or documented in the USA. There must be numerous examples which have gone by unnoticed.

- Were the avenues aligned upon a track line?

- Check the enclosures for a geospiral, primary halo and primary spirals.

- Dowse the area for a power point to locate the cleansing area.

- Is Newark one of 7 major sites symbolically depicting a chakra system, or one of 12 representing a ground-based linear-like zodiac? Some of the sites could include Serpent Mound; Fort Hill near Paint Creek; Hopeton earthworks; Seip earthworks and its companion site Baum earthworks. Bourneville circle was recorded by the antiquarians, Ephraim Squier and Edwin Davis as 'one of the most beautiful in the state of Ohio'. Others may include Sprue hillfort, Chillicothe, Circleville and Newark earthworks.

Alligator Mound

Take a 10-minute drive to Alligator Mound which lies between Granville and Newark on privately owned land at the end of Bryn Du Drive. The mound is about 200 feet (60.96 metres) long and although it is called 'Alligator Mound' Brad Lepper believes it represented a mythological creature known as the 'underwater panther'. Brad thinks that Native Americans described the creature to Europeans who were told that a fierce creature lived in the water and ate people, which they mistakenly interpreted as an alligator.

Dowsing

- Dowse for the crossing of leys which, as we read earlier, intersect at animal effigies.
- Aquastats which may outline the mound.

Serpent Mound, Adams County, Ohio

Serpent Mound is a spectacular earthen effigy 1,348 feet (411 metres) long and 3 feet. (0.91 metres) high, located on a plateau in Adams County, Ohio. Serpent Mound was first reported in surveys by Ephraim Squier and Edwin Davis in their historic volume *Ancient Monuments of the Mississippi Valley* published in 1848 by the newly founded Smithsonian Museum. Recent radiocarbon dates suggest that Serpent Mound was built as many as 2,000 years later than previously thought. The effigy had been attributed to the Adena culture (1000–100 BC) based on the presence of Adena burials nearby. However, two samples of wood charcoal were obtained from undisturbed parts of the mound which yielded a date of 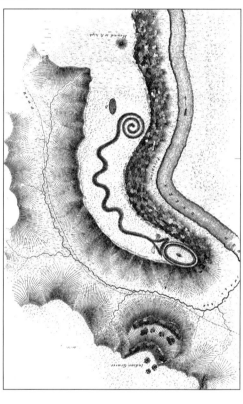 circa 1070 AD. So which date is correct, or is bioturbation causing confusion?

Bioturbation

Bioturbation is a process caused by worms which can produce inaccurate archaeological dating. In 1995 two animal bone experts published the results of a bioturbation experiment they had carried out using a glass fish tank. They filled a fish tank with soil and earthworms and then placed the corpses of two voles and a mouse on its surface. Within 24 weeks the earthworms had scattered the bones throughout the soil, with most bones at a depth of 3 inches (10 centimetres) below the surface and some at depths of more than 7 inches (20 centimetres). The pieces of charcoal used for dating Serpent Mound may well have been repositioned by earthworms. Charles Darwin knew of the process and studied bioturbation and its consequences at Stonehenge.

Serpent Mound is sited in a meteor crater. Many writers suggest that beneath the mound are caverns or hollow structures, so there may be more to the serpent hidden underground. Perhaps the native people knew of the meteor's explosion and constructed the mound to honour the event. Astronomical alignments to the summer solstice sunset and, less clearly, to the winter solstice sunrise were incorporated in the effigy. Other researchers suggest the earthen serpent aligns to the celestial serpent, Draco. If the mound was created at the later date of 1070 AD it may have been a Native American response to unusual celestial events. Light from the supernova that produced the Crab Nebula first reached Earth in 1054 AD and remained visible, even during the day, for two weeks. Also the brightest appearance of Halley's Comet was recorded by Chinese astronomers in 1066 AD which was seen by people worldwide.

Locating earth energies

Many dowsers have located blind springs along the meandering humps of the earthen serpent. These are *branch spirals* which are life enhancing and were incorporated into European Neolithic long barrows and homesteads. British medieval Masons set bedrooms within stately homes, and also barns, above them to ensure continual health, wealth and fertility. Led by David Webb our scientific equipment recorded vast amounts of negative ions above certain

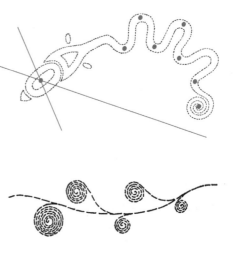

branch spiral coils and invariably a beneficial 7-10 Hz frequency flows along an aquastat stream.

Illinois's healing spiral

Woodhenge is a giant timber circle in the Cahokia complex, Illinois, which contains a geospiral at its near centre. Inspired by our book The Essential Dowsing Guide American dowser and author Robert Egby located the geospiral which is marked by a giant cedar pole. Instantly he felt earth energy coming up from the ground through his feet. The energy spiralled up his legs and body until it reached his head. He clung onto the pole in disbelief! Afterwards his spiritual guides told him that Woodhenge was once a vast Cahokian healing centre. Illnesses were healed, he was told by his guide, within hours by standing over the geospiral whose perimeter is marked by cedar poles.

Ancient sites and the Pentagon

The Pentagon is the headquarters of the United States Department of Defense, located in Arlington County, Virginia. It has five sides, five floors above ground, two basement levels and five ring corridors per floor. The central plaza contains a five-acre area which is shaped like a pentagon and informally known as 'ground zero', a nickname originating during the Cold War and based on the presumption that the Soviet Union would target one or more nuclear missiles at this central location in the outbreak of a nuclear war.

Considering the Pentagon's unusual shape it was designed in just five days by the American architect George Bergstrom (1876-1955) between July 17th and July 22nd 1941. The number '5' features repeatedly in its design. Ground was broken for construction on September 11 1941 and many researchers have wondered how the controversial design was so quickly conceived.

Was the design based on a prehistoric monument unique to North America? Antiquarians surveyed five unusual pentagon earthworks in Wisconsin, which incidentally was the birthplace of George Bergstrom the Pentagon's designer. Without question the pentagon monuments were still intact and visible whilst he was growing up. No where else in the world do we see this type of monumental shape which was constructed around two thousand years ago. The macabre latter-day use of the pentagon earthwork symbolically parallels the modern Pentagon's function and possible agenda.

One outstanding pentagon earthwork was located by the Kickapoo River, about 30 miles (48 kilometres) northeast of Prairie du Chien and consisted of an outer circle enclosing a pentagon, or five-angled walls, with seven truncated mounds of various dimensions, and a small inner circle. One 19th century antiquarian report stated that the earthwork had been 'defaced by the ravages of

time'; however, certain areas within the monument remained 'perfectly intact'. The outer circle was more than 1,200 feet (365.76 metres) in circumference and the earthen wall was around 5 feet (1.52 metres) high with a general base diameter of 12-16 feet (3.65-4.87 metres). However, the small inner circle had diminished to only 12 inches (30.48 centimetres). In contrast the pentagon walls had retained 'a more perfect form'.

The internal central mound was about 36 feet (10.97 metres) in diameter, had a smooth finish and was in excellent condition. According to Dee-Coo-Dah 'this [earthwork] is traditional and was designed for a sacred national altar at which human sacrifice was offered. The central mound was the most holy sacrificial altar known to tradition and the pentagon [earthworks] was the highest order of sacrificial monuments'. Morbidly, the head of a self-appointed victim was the only part offered in the sacrifice and it was a great honour to offer yourself willingly.

The pentagonal earthwork symbolized the head and the five senses of seeing, hearing, feeling, tasting and smelling. An extended interpretation could include the head of the tribe, region or country. The five small mounds within the pentagon were denominated oracular mounds, one for each prophet. They frequently retired there to receive oracular counsels which, from the summit of the mound at the entrance to the great circle, they subsequently delivered to the people. Spectators would stand on the outer wall and throw evergreens into the inner circle watching the sacred procession which had to pass five times in a circular fashion around the pentagon. The five passes represented dominance and the blood ensured the country's strength, power and domination. To foretell the future the prophets had to walk in a circular manner around the inside of the monument five times. Intriguingly, the modern Pentagon has five ring corridors per floor as if mirroring or re-enacting this ancient ritual; coincidence? This grisly rite is far removed from its original purpose, which is still an unsolved mystery. However, this dark symbolism of the pentagon abides. Fifty years after its destruction it was resurrected as the Pentagon. Prophets have been replaced by remote viewers, and the latter-day use of the pentagon earthwork and the modern military version are undeniably both associated with the spilling of blood.

The earthen pentagon represented the head of state, strength and power as does the modern day pentagon. The oracular prophecies foretold future events creating an advantageous position when used by the seer or the warrior.

Crop circles

Genuine crop circles emit energy as well as orientating themselves on leys and earth energies.

Dowsing crop circles

Dowse a crop circle for:

- Geospirals which are never at the exact geometric centre.
- Primary concentric haloes as these often set the location and size of circular monuments.
- Power points generating vortex energy.
- Serpentine Genesis leys.
- Dowse your aura before and after interacting with the crop circle to ascertain if the energy influences the subtle bodies.

Nodal points

When dragon lines cross they form a node. A node is where the earth energy penetrates the ground deeply and emerges a short distance away. Nodal points are exceptionally powerful places and in ancient China were exclusively reserved for the Emperor's temples, tombs and palaces. They are excellent locations for meditation, inspiration and intuitive insight. Nodes can create a sense of deep awareness. Over the years I have noted that many people who are at a crossroads in life, confused or unsure of their path, receive a strong sense or a vision of their spiritual purpose upon a nodal point.

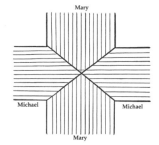

Dowsing nodal points

Locate the outer edge of a dragon line and track it towards a crossing point. You will notice that it begins to turn inwards directing you to the node. Use the map of the Elen and Belinus dragon currents at the Rollright Ring to locate and experience a powerful node point. Dowse alongside a friend on either side of the line and you will both meet in the middle!

Greece. The Acropolis, Athens

In 1962 Guy Underwood studied the Acropolis in Athens and his survey is published for the first time. It reveals the geodetic energies that were skilfully integrated into the temple's foundation plans. Many dowsers including life-long dowser Sir Charles Jessel, past president and honorary life vice president of the British Society of Dowsers, have confirmed Underwood's original findings at Greece.

The Temple of Athena Nike was built between 427 and 424 BC and was erected on top of the remains of an earlier 6th century BC temple dedicated to Athena. A statue of Nike stood in the *cella* above an emerging aquastat energy line, imbuing the statue with living energy. Nike was originally the 'winged victory' goddess; however, the Athena Nike statue was wingless and led to Athenians in later centuries to call it *Nike Apteros*, 'wingless victory', and the story arose that the statue was deprived of wings so that it could never leave the city.

Dowsing the Acropolis

Spectacular energy patterns can be dowsed at the Temple of Nike. The survey 'A' shows that the pillars are set by concentric flows and at 'B' the inner dimensions are set by the triple concentric haloes within which is a powerful geospiral. The entrance points of the temple have parallel energy flows passing through them from the geospiral. Decreeing a sacred processional way to enter the monument, the aquastats generate an attractive force field dedicated to the feminine principle.

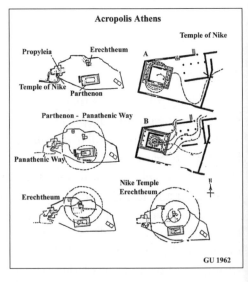

Energy is drawn upwards by the site's elevation

The Parthenon is a temple dedicated to the maiden goddess Athena whom the people of Athens considered their patron deity. Temple construction began in 447 BC when the Athenian Empire was at the height of its power and it took nine years to complete. It is the most important surviving building of Classical Greece and is regarded as an enduring symbol of Ancient Greece, Athenian democracy and Western civilization. Like most Greek temples the Parthenon was also used as a treasury and in the 5th century AD, the Parthenon was converted into a Christian church dedicated to the Virgin Mary. After the Ottoman conquest it was turned into a mosque in the early 1460s. Interestingly, the temple is aligned to the Hyades – one of the dragon constellations.

The Panathenaic Way was named after a procession which took place during the summer festival of Panathenaia. The forked Panathenaic Way south of the Propyleia is set by geodetic track lines and the Parthenon is ringed by an ovoid flow. From the right fork of the Panathenaic Way the energy flow continues in an easterly direction, enters the Parthenon's east face and ends within a spiral. It actually splits and another flow line enters the Erechtheum and, likewise, terminates in a spiral.

Dowsing aquastat primary spirals

When aquastats form primary spirals they split into two lines, one half forms a spiral and the other half proceeds to the geospiral. The two halves reunite at the geospiral as shown in the illustration. You can dowse for this geodetic phenomenon at the near centre of Avebury's southern inner circle or by the Heel Stone at Stonehenge. The aquastatic spiral is healing and protective.

Stanton Drew Stone Circles, Somerset

Stanton Drew stone circle is the second largest stone circle in England. The megalithic complex consists of three stone circles. In the nearby pub garden of the appropriately named 'Druid's Arms' are the remains of a megalithic Cove feature – similar to the Cove feature at Avebury Henge in Wiltshire. Recently geophysical analysis of the Cove suggests it may be the remains of a long barrow. The Cove stones were sited over a gigantic 21-coiled geospiral. Cove features create an enclosed area within a vast megalithic complex and, as we have seen, Avebury's Cove had a stone floor and was deemed a healing area. Possibly Stanton Drew's cove was similarly designed.

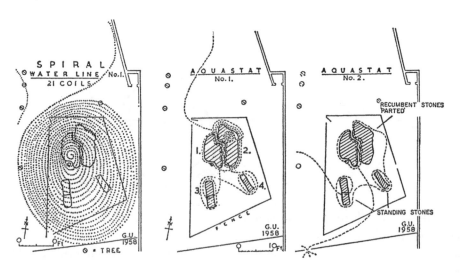

The Cove, Stanton Drew
Survey Guy Underwood 1958

- Dowse for the individual coils of the geospiral at the Cove. They are grouped tightly together creating an intense aquastatic enclosure that pulsates energy in rhythmic fashion. This type of geospiral is all-powerful.

- Detect the aquastat lines that flow around the Cove stones – you will get 12 hairlines of energy depicting the width of the energy line. You need to dowse exceptionally slowly to achieve definition of the hairlines.

- The stone avenue, which leads to the River Chew, has an aquastat line flowing either side of the avenue marking its course and a water line flows down the centre creating a holy line. Locate the line/s by crossing the avenue at right angles and then track them individually.

- Sense the energy as you walk or stand upon the line. How does the holy line energy make you feel? Close your eyes, what colour do you perceive?

Trethevy Quoit, Cornwall.

Trethevy Quoit in Cornwall is associated with several primary spirals making this sacred space ideal for any type of psychic work. The spirals give protective sanctity to the monument. Other earth energies such as the Mary earth energy current also flows through the stones. Sited close to a 3.5 geospiral which corresponds to the base chakra, this site may have been associated with the raising of kundalini in the body and the land.

Druid centres and Celtic crosses

Celtic Iron Age hill forts majestically crown the summits of numerous hills across Britain and Europe. Not all hill forts were defensive and some served as ceremonial centres. This is reinforced by the fact that the towering earthen banks originally appeared chalk-white making the enclosure visible for miles, not a strategic warfare tactic. Previously I mentioned that the harmonic crossing points of aquastats are invariably found within Celtic ceremonial enclosures denoting temple space and healing areas.

The Celtic cross chimney

I have also detected other dowsable patterns within the Druid centres which I call the 'Celtic cross chimney' and believe that it was revered by the Druid priesthood as it sanctified a magico-religious area. When the geo-chimney pattern manifests four arms and a simple enclosing circle it is reminiscent of the early Celtic religious symbol. When this geodetic configuration is found on high ground it is exceptionally powerful and creates a cosmic-telluric connection – a celestial portal.

At Druid centres dowse for

- Harmonic crossing points and the inward spirals
- Celtic cross earth chimneys
- How do the two energies compare?

Old Sarum, Salisbury, Wiltshire

Old Sarum is a stunning Iron Age hill fort which is dominated by a Norman motte. Echoes of the past can be easily found and dowsed within the grounds: the foundations of an old castle, cathedral and bishop's palace dating to circa 1068-1078 AD. The hill fort has a simple bank and ditch with an entrance in the east. Archaeological finds include storage pits, pottery and several brooches. Old Sarum

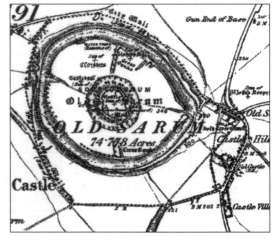

may have been the location for the Roman station of Sorviodunum,

- Dowse for the long-gone cloisters as shown in the illustration
- Dowse for a ley which courses from Salisbury Cathedral to Old Sarum and on to Stonehenge.
- Locate a Celtic cross geo-chimney within the grounds
- Dowse for a powerful ionic vortex

The Devil's Den, near Marlborough, Wiltshire

Five miles (8 kilometres) east of Avebury, near the old market town of Marlborough, stands a Welsh-style dolmen called The Devil's Den. Dolmen chambers consist of 2, 3 or 4 vertical megaliths supporting a capstone megalith.

In the 1920s archaeologists suggested that the Devil's Den was the remains of a long barrow burial chamber that was once 229 feet (70 metres) long and 131 feet (40 metres) wide which faced South-East – North-West. Richard Atkinson and Stuart Piggott carried out an excavation of the site and found nothing – not one bone. Today archaeologists see the dolmen as a style of monument which was sited on an earthen mound. In 2011 a geophysical survey revealed the remains of a second mound immediately to the north of it which may be the remains of another long-lost dolmen.

Guy Underwood surveyed the monument in 1958 and produced a remarkable survey. Sited over 6 geospirals of 35 and 49 coils the monument marked a geodetic power centre. This geospiral configuration occurs when large pockets of underground water are sited close to one another but at various different depths. According to our long-term research the energy creates a vast amount of rotating electromagnetic energy which generates an intense concentric circular energy field. Further investigations concluded

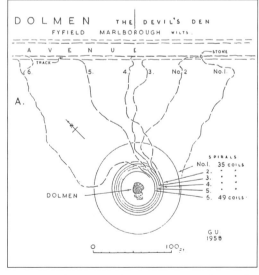

that this type of earth energy configuration pulsates earth energy *away* from the site, and this phenomenon is called 'energy irrigation'.

Auspicious horseshoes

To ancient geomancers the energy emitted
by a meandering current, be that a surface
river, road or energy flow, was especially
auspicious when it bends to form a loop or
horseshoe shape. Working with the land
and earth energies we can create harmonic
spaces that reconnect us to Gaia. The
survey of the five trilithons at Stonehenge
by Guy Underwood in the 1950s revealed
a horseshoe energy flow personifying
sacred space.

Callanish, Isle of Lewis, Western Isles, Scotland

Callanish is one of the wonders of Scotland. On the Isle of Lewis stands
a stone circle in the shape of a Celtic Cross. Lewis is a timeless landscape
that is intimately associated with the moon. Every 18.61 years its rising
awakens the sleeping mountain goddess known as *Cailleach as Monteach*
or the *Old Woman of the Moors*. The mountain peaks and valleys create
a recumbent goddess figure often refereed to as *Sleeping Beauty*. Every
18.6 years the moon rises and slowly moves along the contours of the
great goddess, gently arousing the energies of the land amid the silence
of the night. As the moon begins to set it aligns with the centre of the
Callanish stone circle and creates a sight to behold. At this latitude, so
low on the horizon, and so large the moon, it has been calculated that a

person standing with outstretched hands at the circle's centre would appear to be *in the moon* to spectators looking from one of the stone avenues. This is because the moon's South Extreme is at a distance of about 574 feet (175 metres); the person and the moon subtend to the same angle. Margaret Curtis is a world authority on the moon and Callanish and she is the must-have guide when visiting the Callanish landscape.

Rainbow colours rising high

The energies of Callanish are unique. The central geospiral is like no other. Long-term studies have shown that the tight coils of the 42-coiled geospiral emit all the earth colours in rotation. The geospiral energy can also be experienced rising out of the ground and rotating around the stone circle as the stones and the energy merge as one. Please remember that earth energies are not 2-D as shown in the illustrations in this book but are 3-D creating an Earthgate to the 4th dimension and beyond.

- Dowse the coils, all of which are exceptionally close.
- The stones are set precisely on the geospiral which produces an extraordinary phenomenon. The spiral energy rises out of the ground and passes between the stones. Tune into the energy, begin with a rod close to the ground and then slowly raise the rod upwards. When one of the aerial coils has been detected the rod will swing into the 'found' position.
- Feel the energy with your hand – you will experience an amazing sensation.

In these Isles the Goddess is all around. The Outer Hebrides are named after the Great Celtic Goddess Brigid. She is the Giver of Plenty and the teacher of skills. At Callanish it is said that if you ask the goddess for advice or healing she will hear you as she listens to every sound that moves on the wind and water. Within the centre of the stone circle gently ask Brigid for that which you need.

In the late 1980s a crop circle resembling the Callanish stone circle appeared in the Wessex landscape. Pioneer crop circle photographer Busty Taylor has kindly granted permission to use his photograph which shows the likeness.

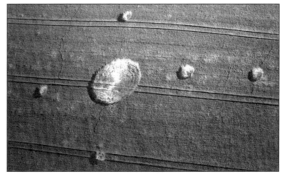

Meet Herne

Etched into one of the Callanish Stones is the Celtic deity Herne the Hunter. I took this photograph of Herne in 2006 during the 18.61 year cycle and instantly the camera screen poured with white light – like a flash of iridescent light which touched my hand. The camera never worked again but I felt the magic of Herne that day! Look carefully at the photograph and you will see a tall figure with a large body and antlers on his head – this is Herne of Callanish; a true aspect of Nature, magic and sacred Celtic lore.

The Ring of Brodgar, Orkney, Scotland.

The Orkney Isles offer some of the most ancient and spectacular temple spaces in the United Kingdom. The stone circle known as the Ring of Brodgar is a near-complete stone circle. Dowse for 'form energy' that the shape of a circle produces which is described in *The Essential Dowsing Guide* as here it is especially strong due to the close proximity of water. One summer solstice I was waiting for the sunrise but heavy cloud obscured the sun. I asked photographer Busty Taylor where the sun should be on the horizon line and took a photograph. Although the sun was not visible, in its exact position was a bright orb as if mimicking the sun.

Orbrise at the Ring of Brodgar

APPENDIX 1
Dowsing made simple - some professional tips

For those that have never dowsed I recommend *The Essential Dowsing Guide* by Dennis Wheatley which explores dowsing fundamentals. However, I will outline the basic dowsing principles so that anyone who reads this book can pick up a dowsing rod and experience the Earth Force.

Dowsing is a natural 'sixth sense' latent in all of us which can be easily triggered and, with practice, developed to professional standards. But before we explore the simple dowsing precepts let us look at the dowsing tools. Over 3,000 dowsing tools have been defined, but we will concentrate only on the most popular tools, the metal L-rod and pendulums.

L-rods

Rods can be bought or made from metal coat-hangers, piano wire or fence wire bent into an L-shape with the handling end being about 5-6 inches (12.5-15 centimetres) with the long end around 10-15 inches (25-30 centimetres). A sleeve, such as a biro pen casing, can be attached to the handling end and this eliminates skin friction and allows the rods to swivel easily.

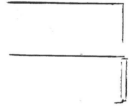

Pendulums

A pendulum is simply a weight from 0.08-0.35 ounces (2.5-10 grams) attached to a twine, cord or fine chain. The material of the bob can be wood, plastic, metal or crystal. It can be homemade, purchased at shops or bought online.

Rod holding

Hold the rods in a 'pistol-type' grip with the upper and lower arms at right-angles to each other. The rods should be held apart at body width and should be parallel to each other and the ground. This is the 'search' or 'prospecting' mode. On passing over or through a target the rods will swing into 'found' mode. This varies with individuals. For some the rods will swing inwardly to cross each other by 45 degrees or may even swing in by some 90 degrees, coming to rest along the body. For others the rods may swing apart by 90 degrees as if repulsing each other.

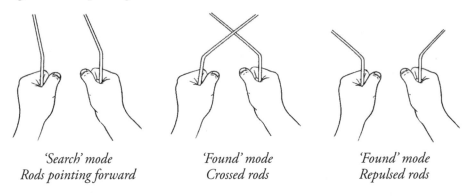

'Search' mode
Rods pointing forward

'Found' mode
Crossed rods

'Found' mode
Repulsed rods

Accuracy reference point

To locate the target accurately one needs an accuracy reference point. This could be the tip of the right thumb. If you select this reference point then simply command the rods to swing to 'found' when the thumb tip is aligned with the target. Now make another dowsing pass across a selected target and note that the rods respond as the position of your thumb tip coincides with the target. Your practice target could be the edge of a table or path. When dowsing in the landscape I use the tip of my right foot as my accuracy reference point.

Visualization

Dowsing can be described as finding invisible targets by deploying the sixth sense. The first principle of dowsing is that we cannot find that which we cannot visualize. So visualization is important. A dowsing great, the late Hamish Miller, believed that with correct visualization the scope of dowsing is 'virtually infinite'. We can easily visualize, for example, underground utilities such as water pipes and gas pipes or underground cables, and lost articles such as car keys, wallets etc. Underground fissured streams, likewise, can be easily visualized. But how do you visualize earth energies or leys? Earth energies, geodetic flows, and leys can be visualized, for example, as a meandering silver energy flow or a straight silver line. Geospirals can be similarly visualized as a silver coil on the Earth's surface. Use whatever form of visualization best suits you.

Frame of mind

Accurate dowsing requires the right 'frame of mind' which can be easily attained by mastering a few simple precepts.

- Relax, bodily and mentally; take a couple of deep breaths and let your arms hang loosely by your sides.
- Eliminate all butterfly thoughts; still the mind; bury the ego.
- Visualize the target in quiet concentration. But, importantly, do not 'over-concentrate' as this will lead either to no results or, at best, spurious results.
- Be quietly confident that the rods will work for you, but never be over-confident. Dowsing cockiness produces inconsistent results!
- Eliminate from the mind all preconceived notions, biases, autosuggestion; and **never** predict what the rods will do. **Should you do this the rods will willingly oblige by reacting as you predicted.**
- Should a sudden noise interrupt your dowsing 'frame of mind' – a passing car, helicopter or voices – abandon the dowsing pass and re-establish your 'frame of mind'.
- Don't be over-serious about dowsing. It's great fun, so enjoy it!

In the precepts described we are faced with an apparent contradiction in talking of 'relaxation' and 'concentration' simultaneously. Hamish Miller neatly sums up dowsing in his phrase 'relaxed concentration'.

Dowsing can be fatiguing so dowse in short periods followed by relaxation breaks. A suitable routine could be, for example, fifteen minutes dowsing with a ten-minute relaxation break. If you visit an ancient site to dowse for say, earth energies, do not begin dowsing immediately. If you have journeyed by car you will probably be stressed. Each site has its own 'persona' or 'spirit of place' so, on arrival, relax for fifteen minutes and quietly absorb the ambience and feel of the place.

Information dowsing

Rods can be programmed to give 'yes' or 'no' responses. Simply put the rods into 'search' and give the polite command 'Show me a "yes" response'. Repeat the procedure with 'Show me a "no" response'. As in establishing your 'found' mode, the rods will decide for you what these responses are; for example, crossed rods for 'yes' and repulsed rods for 'no', or vice-versa. Once established these responses will be constant for the rest of your life but, at this stage, you must heed a caveat. The rods can act capriciously for reasons unknown and occasionally will switch the yes/no responses for a day or so and then revert back to the original mode. Unless this is recognized you could invoke spurious answers. So, a vital rule in 'information dowsing' is that, prior to seeking answers, you must always check that your original yes/no responses prevail. It only takes a matter of seconds to confirm a 'yes' response.

With rods programmed to give 'yes' and 'no' responses one can enter the infinite world of information dowsing, answering questions even of an abstract nature, finding lost objects or seeking directions. Imagine all of the possible questions your mind can conjure up. You could, as a first experiment, begin by laying down a line of household commodities such as an apple, boot polish, a pear, furniture polish, fruit juice, bread, detergent powder, cheese and washing-up liquid, then asking the question at each item 'Is this commodity capable of being easily digested by me?' Note the answers.

Were they correct? Repeat the exercise until you are fully confident.

Trick answers

So far we have examined several pitfalls in dowsing, from over-concentration to over-confidence and the loss of that all-important aspect, the correct 'frame of mind'. In 'relaxed concentration' we must realize that it is up to ourselves to create that sense of 'balance' in concentration and confidence, but the capricious rods may enter into the dowsing equation in more ways than one. We now recognize that our constant yes/no responses can switch, sporadically and transiently, but what if the rods provide 'trick' answers? How would we identify an answer as being true or false? Do the rods really have a mind of their own and revel in the taming of egos?

Tom Graves, one of the most prolific authors on dowsing, recognized this trait in rods and pendulums and called trick answers 'Hermes responses'! Hermes was one of the Olympian gods and amongst his many talents was trickery. So, how does one sort out the true from the false? Simply use information dowsing and ask the question 'Is this a trick response?' and note the answer - *'Yes, this is a trick response'*, or *'No, it is not!'* Once they have been rumbled the rods will come clean! So, with these examples of a rod's capriciousness, it behoves us not to have unbridled faith in the dowsing instruments, be they rods or pendulums, and always check responses. Verify a response once only. As an experiment I tried verifying a questionable response several times and received the 'yes' reply four times. On the fifth time the rods suddenly reverted to 'no'. It is as if the rods had wearied of this constant probing and, eventually, decided to confuse persistent questioners. They have a short fuse in toleration.

A prerequisite to dowsing

There is one more essential requirement for successful dowsing. Dowsing accuracy requires a 'balanced' state of being – physically, mentally and emotionally. If you are 'unbalanced' you may receive inaccurate dowsing responses, not because of the rod's capricious nature but because of your own energies!

Prior to any dowsing task I recommend that you check that you are 'balanced'. For instance, colds, feeling low and a lack of sleep can have an unbalancing effect. However, you may not always notice that you are emotionally or mentally 'unbalanced', so it is always a good idea to check and it only takes a few seconds.

- Check that your 'yes' and 'no' responses prevail (dowsing rods or pendulum).
- Place one hand over, or close to, the solar plexus chakra (standing or sitting position).
- Hold a dowsing instrument in the free hand and simply ask the question: *'Am I in balance'*?
- If the answer is 'yes' proceed with the dowsing task.
- If you are out of balance you could relax, meditate, smudge the aura or take a few drops of Bach flower rescue remedy to encourage the mind, body and spirit to harmonize.

Ask the right question

The art of successful dowsing is, simply, asking the right question. Always try to make the question short, crystal clear and never ask double answer questions such as, for example, 'Is X big and black?' What is big – an elephant, a planet, a star or a galaxy? If size is important, relate the question to metric or imperial measurement units. 'Is X over 500 metres in depth?' 'Yes'. 'Is it over 800 metres in depth?' 'No'. So it is in between, and now you can home in on the depth. 'Is it 510, 520, 530 metres?' And so on. Suppose you wish to know a standing stone's date of erection. If you ask the question 'How old is this stone?' and start counting backwards from, say, 1000 BC in units of 50 years...1050,

1100, 1150, etc., be prepared to stand around for weeks or months on end as the stone may have had its genesis countless millions of years ago! The correct question would be: 'When was this stone placed in this location?' If you ask a vague, ill-defined question do not expect a crystal-clear answer.

Rod reactions in count exercises

In counting exercises the rods are held in the 'search' mode. As the counting proceeds the rods will remain in 'search' but as the target count is nearest the rods swing inwardly by a few degrees. This means you are getting close! Keep on counting and the rods will gradually inch nearer to the 'found' position when the correct count is reached.

Pendulum dowsing

A pendulum can also be programmed to give yes/no responses in information dowsing. One method of achieving this is to sit on a chair in an upright position and relax. Hold the pendulum cord at a length that 'feels' right for you. This could be 5, 2, 3, 4 or 5 inches (7.5, 10, or 12.5 centimetres). Position the pendulum bob so that it is around 1 inch (2.5 centimetres) or so above the right kneecap which is a minor 'chakra' point. Now set the pendulum bob in a 'search' swing, that is to say a forward and backward linear oscillation with a swing length of around 3 to 4 inches (7.5 to 10 centimetres). Now give the quiet command: 'Show me a "yes" response'. The search swing may continue for a short period and then the bob will produce a 'yes' response. My 'yes' response is a clockwise swing. The 'no' response can be found by repeating the procedure over the left kneecap.

These simple dowsing tips will open up a new dimension where you will be able to detect and directly experience the Earth's invisible energy system. Have fun interacting with earth energies. It's a magical experience!

Sensing underground yang water

Instead of using a dowsing rod to locate an underground stream you can use your body, hands or feet and this is called 'deviceless dowsing'. Have a go at deviceless dowsing as it will help you to understand the subtle frequencies of earth energy. Locate an underground stream with a dowsing rod and spend some time standing or sitting upon the stream to get a *feel* of its energy – its energetic signature. How does it make you feel and what do you sense? Now, slowly walk across the stream and make a note of any body sensations or feelings you experience.

Some people find that walking across the stream with their left arm outstretched and the palm facing downwards towards the earth enhances awareness. Can you feel anything in your hand as you cross the stream? For me, underground water can often make my hand feel cold and I get a particular feeling when in close proximity to underground water. This is how I detect its energetic signature *before* I begin to dowse.

Sensing yin water/aquastats

Stand or sit on the aquastat energy for a short period of time to get a feel of its energetic signature and notice how it makes you feel. Slowly walk across or along the energy flow and make a note of any body sensations or feelings you experience.

Try using your right hand to detect the aquastat. Walk towards the energy with the right arm outstretched and the palm of your right hand facing downwards towards the earth. Can you feel anything in your hand as you cross the aquastat? For me, aquastats can often make my hand feel warm and I get a particular feeling when in close proximity to this uplifting energy. By recognizing how a particular energy makes you feel will help you to interpret a landscape or property. Try interacting with other forms of earth energy and explore how they, too, make you feel.

Activating your earthstar chakra

A geomantic connection to the Earth is important as it can enhance our sensitivity to earth energies creating a bridge between the Earth and us. One way to genuinely understand the Earth and heighten your dowsing awareness is to open the earthstar chakra. The earthstar chakra is often refereed to as a transpersonal chakra which is located a few inches beneath your feet. This powerful chakra point connects you to the vast planetary body of Earth and all of her kingdoms, wisdom and love. During my dowsing courses I encourage people to activate/open their earthstar chakra, which is a truly profound experience. Once this chakra is consciously opened in the name of divine love, you will have a deep and lasting connection to Gaia and her energies.

To activate the earthstar chakra I suggest choosing a place that makes you feel good. Places that make us feel good naturally raise our frequencies to a higher level and make ideal activation spots. Or I suggest sacred space marked by an earth energy pattern such as a geospiral or primary spiral which personifies a healing and protective space. Use your own guidance to show you where to activate/open this chakra and only open this chakra when you are feeling positive and grounded.

At your given location close your eyes and surround yourself with love and golden light. Feel the Earth beneath your feet and sense the connection that you have with the Earth. Ask the Earth Mother's permission to connect to her infinite love and wisdom and sense your request being received. Now give thanks and send the Earth love and gratitude for all her life forms. Think of the animal, mineral and plant kingdoms and all the wondrous diverse forms of life that live upon the Earth. Send love and light to all life forms including the unseen kingdoms of light beings, devas and the elementals, and sense your love being received. Now just remain in love, gratitude and openness...

In the stillness of time you may experience something truly profound. Many people who have activated their earthstar chakra tell me they have felt joyous as they sense a deep connection to the Earth naturally occurring. One person told me that after the activation she opened her eyes and saw in the sky clouds of silver and gold. Most people say they feel a true and divine connection to the Earth and to all life forms that words cannot express. Each experience is unique and personal, whether you see colours or simply feel joyous; connecting to Gaia is a truly remarkable experience and one that you will cherish for the rest of your life.

APPENDIX 2
The Geodetic Rod

Guy Underwood invented a highly sensitive dowsing instrument called the geodetic rod and I have a small supply of these innovative rods which are a part of dowsing history. Email me if you wish to obtain one. Many dowsers find the geodetic rod difficult to handle and, admittedly, the L-rod is much easier to use. Nonetheless, Guy was a forward thinker and realized that geodetic energies influenced different sides of the body. Reacting to the slightest energy change in the earth the geodetic rod is highly sensitive creating a bridge between you and the Earth's energy system. The following article on how to use the geodetic rod for water divining was written by Guy. Without his geodetic rod and his deep awareness of the Earth's whispering energies we would never have known about the geospiral, haloes or aquastats and I feel very privileged to have worked with Guy's material and I am honoured to pass his wisdom on.

Instructions wfor the Geodetic Rod and Notes on Water Divining by the late, great, Guy Underwood

Many people are familiar with the village water-finder and his forked stick cut from a hedge. This stick is called the 'dowser's twig' and by its use he locates water supplies for farmers and others. He seldom fails.

Only a limited number of people are able to use the dowser's twig and the power to do so appears to depend on a physiological peculiarity of such persons. The geodetic rod is intended for use by ordinary people who are not natural water-diviners and are unable to use the dowser's twig. The majority will find that it will work satisfactorily in their hands.

Hold the rod as shown in the illustration on page 146. Grasp the handle very firmly in the left hand for water divining (and a right-hand is required for aquastats, track lines, and a lighter right-hand grip for geospirals, haloes, and arcs). Press strongly on the link with the flexible rod, keeping the link balanced on the handle.

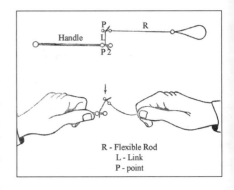

R - Flexible Rod
L - Link
P - point

Note: the right thumb should be about 2 inches (5 centimetres) from the link and the left thumb close to the other end of it. The link should be approximately the angle to the handle shown in the illustration otherwise it may jam.

Before attempting water divining practice doing this while standing still and increase the pressure until the link cannot be balanced any longer and flicks over.

When in use the pressure on the link should be strong, but a little less will upset the equilibrium. Now walk forward with the link nearly horizontal, pointing forward and slightly downward, keeping it balanced at the same angle and at the same pressure and as steady as possible.

Action of the rod

On crossing an underground stream the point 'P' will dip three times strongly and regain its original position after each dip. This is the water reaction. The stream will be found vertically beneath. *(Editor: For me, the point 'P' dips down but does not regain its original position and so I reset it and continue the dowsing pass. If you are using an L-rod hold it firmly in the left hand.)* Note: the rod will waver as the dowser walks along, but these waverings are clearly distinguishable from the dips of the water reaction. The latter are much stronger and more definite. Each 'dip' usually causes the link to make a half circle round the handle.

Tracking

When a water reaction has been located the dowser can follow its course by crossing it diagonally and repeatedly, getting the triple water reaction each time.

[When divining aquastats which are the most important geodetic lines in the design layout of an ancient site, tune into the energy by visualizing an underground stream flowing as a lavender or white coloured stream. You will get six dowsing reactions, followed by a larger gap then another six reactions].

Notes on water divining

Water divining is an unsolved mystery. Many people deny its existence. Its reputation has suffered as much from its friends as its enemies – the over-statements of the former having provided ample ammunition for the latter. Its best witnesses are the farmers, who, when they want water, almost invariably employ a diviner and are seldom unsuccessful.

This is well illustrated by my first contact with water diviners. A small country town [Bradford-Upon-Avon] was becoming short of water and it was necessary periodically to reduce supplies, causing much inconvenience. The town lay in a valley among the hills of limestone in which it was supposed that there was plenty of water. A geological survey was made, but much to our surprise no place could be pointed out where a well could be put down with any reasonable prospect of obtaining the water we required.

We approached neighbouring local authorities but they could not help us as they were all nearly as short of water as we were.

We found ourselves in a difficult position. If we could not find water on our own land we had only two alternatives, either bring water from a distance, at a cost that would have crippled the finances of the town for generations or, secondly, take water from the river which ran through the town. However, periodically, hundreds of dead or dying fish floated bottom upwards, evidently poisoned. We had no wish that our constitutions should sufferer in a similar way.

Public bodies are reluctant to employ water diviners except as a last resort. They have to think of their dignity. The last thing they like is ridicule. Many people regard water divining as a supernatural phenomenon. It has a faint imaginary aroma of witchcraft. However, a water diviner was brought over and he selected a spot at the bottom of the valley close to the river where he said there was a good supply. He would not commit himself further than this and appeared unable to tell us how deep we should have to go.

The selected spot seemed unlikely and unsatisfactory. We therefore engaged another diviner to find, if possible, a more convincing but equally good site elsewhere. This diviner made a wide survey and pointed out a number of places where, he said, ample supplies existed, but at great depth. In the end he said he could find no better site than the first, where the water was at only 40 feet (12.18 metres) from the surface, and where he thought it probable that there was enough for our minimum requirements of 1,500 gallons per hour.

We therefore – still with reluctance – sank our well into the rock on the chosen spot. It was completely dry until, at a depth of 37 feet (11.27 metres), a water-bearing fissure was struck which produced a marvellous supply of over ten thousand gallons per hour of perfectly pure water.

This well has been pumped almost continuously, day and night, for fifteen years (bored mid-1940s) without sign of decrease. It rid us of our water difficulties and enabled about 250 more houses to be built which could not otherwise have been done.

This remarkable result somewhat shook my scepticism. Something important and significant had been achieved, greatly to the public benefit, and apparently by means rejected as imaginary by scientists. It might, however, have been a lucky shot by the dowsers and it seemed worthwhile to make some enquiry. I was unable to verify it personally as at that time I could not use the dowser's twig.

Ultimately, I found that if rods of extreme thinness were used they would work in my hands and I was able to locate streams elsewhere which were duly confirmed by more competent dowsers. It is obvious that the twig cannot move automatically; however, it may look or feel to the dowser that it does so. If, as he asserts, he does not move it intentionally then it must be due to some involuntarily movement by him – in other words to a reflex action. It follows that the divining rod is merely an indicator of these reflex movements.

The problem was therefore to find some implement which would exaggerate and make my small reflex movements perceptible. After many experiments this was achieved. A rod evolved which was as lively and prompt as the twig; responded to very weak influences; would rotate, which is an essential property of all efficient divining rods; was reasonably steady in use; and could be used successfully by most people. It also slipped conveniently into the pocket, and its use in public places was not unduly noticeable. I call this implement the geodetic rod and it is with rods of this type that my investigations into the dowsing influence have been made.

Geodetic expertise

Unlike modern-day dowsers Guy did not use information dowsing or the 'show me' dowsing technique. He was guided by geodetic energies and their geometries and concluded that ancient man sought theses patterns and placed monuments upon them. Always led by the Earth's distinct energies, Guy let the landscape speak to him, by doing so he located lost site after lost site by following geodetic energy line flows. Repeatedly, the flows would lead him to the three-fold pattern of the geospiral, primary and secondary halo, the sacred design canon of the ancient world. Energy lines leading to this pattern would invariably mark a processional way, be that of sphinxes as in ancient Egypt, or of standing stones as in Great Britain.

His method was extremely accurate. In 1948 he located an extraordinary Bronze Age round barrow called Jugs Grave, in Farleigh Wick, near Bath.

Geodetic lines flowed towards the barrow and encircled the mound as if protecting the sacred from the profane outer regions. Further dowsing revealed the barrow was crossed by two powerful geodetic lines. Barrow placement upon this energy configuration is rare and Guy thought it may have been reserved for a special individual or possibly royalty. His hunch proved correct as he unearthed one of the country's most treasured gold finds, a so-called Sun disk, a circular object engraved

with a cross. Intriguingly the 'cross' motif on the Sun disk mirrored perfectly the geodetic lines like an exquisite map. Guy spent many decades dowsing geodetic lines of force and he produced hundreds of archaeological and geodetic surveys of sacred sites across Europe. Thankfully so, as he not only saved the round barrows at the western end of the Cursus monument near Stonehenge from the plough but mapped out sites that were sadly ploughed to oblivion.

Recently archaeologists have found Neolithic and Bronze Age roads and track ways. Previously it was wrongly assumed that the Romans introduced road building to England. Guy was the first archaeologist to unearth a prehistoric paved road which he located by dowsing a narrow track line.

My own studies into the geodetic system have spanned over 18 years and I have furthered Guy's work, discovered the significance of the aquastat, the power of crossing aquastats and their distinctive healing pattern. At times I have felt the presence of my late father who I know is guiding me. He smoked a certain brand of tobacco with a strong aroma. Whilst looking for one of Guy's megalithic sites close to Jug's Grave, I was about to give up as hours

of searching had proved futile. Busty Taylor and I returned to the car feeling the entire afternoon had been a waste of time. Suddenly the car filled with the smell of tobacco and I realised this was a sign not to give up! Busty and I looked again with renewed enthusiasm and found the standing stone we had been searching for! Whilst writing this book I have felt Guy around me too and

I have tried hard to interpret his work accurately. His original book *The Pattern of the Past* was published after his death and my late father realised the wrong manuscript had been published. Dad went though all of his manuscripts and matched his writing to the correct and latest survey. We spent hours at sacred sites to test out his theories rather than blindly agree with them. Guy was right. The Earth produces exotic patterns and lines of force that animals recognize and ancient man revered. I truly hope that they are both pleased with this book and with our experiments which prove the existence of the Earth Force they knew so well.

APPENDIX 3
Analysing Earth Energies,
by David Webb, Britain's foremost authority on electromagnetic pollution

Measuring natural earth energies using electronic test equipment was the object of this survey. These sites were previously located by dowsers. First, one needed to differentiate between electromagnetic fields generated from man-made sources and natural fields. Tests were carried out just above ground level and also a little below the ground surface over known anomalies detected by dowsers.

Man-made signals

With ever increasing electromagnetic pollution from wireless communications and the National Grid it is essential to first ensure it was not going to interfere with the experiments. Most of Avebury and the Rollright stones were relatively free of electromagnetic pollution and low-power-density signals from distant microwave transmitters would be evenly distributed over the source and control areas, so unlikely to present a problem. 50 Hz fields (man-made fields) were absent. We were looking for variations between the source (earth energy points) and controls (a neutral area close by) and whether any readings remain stable over time.

One also needs to take into account nearby stone structures, metal fences, gates, power cables, trees and other obstacles that may interfere with delicate measurements. Trees carry their own energy fields and ground microwave signals, whilst metal conducts and deflects as with stone. Apparently many of the foundations under Avebury's standing stones now contain concrete and possibly metal.

The instruments used during these tests consisted of ion counter, field mill, (electrostatic fields) magnetometers, volt meter, Geiger counter, frequency counter 10 Hz – 2.5 GHz, RF field meters 10 MHz – 6+ GHz, (Power density) ELF field meter and 10MHz spectrum analyzer. (Generally using the lower of 17 frequency ranges.)

The experiments

Avebury, Wiltshire, was the first port of call where Maria Wheatley pointed out specific spots located by the late Guy Underwood and her late father both of whom had dowsed and charted a number of ancient sites many years before.

The first test points were small diameter vortices which made things easy. Those spots were named "Power Points" and were discovered by the late Dennis Wheatley. Our experiments began during July 2009 and the variations between the source and controls on a number of other sites were fairly consistent when experiments were repeated.

Avebury 2009

The first experiments at Avebury were over several earth energy points known for their energetic behaviour. During July 2009 anomalies at seven separate locations were detected using the ion counter, and after returning the following month retesting the same sites using the spectrum analyser with voltmeter found small but consistent voltage variations. Over time several types of electrodes were placed below and above the ground surface along with several antenna systems just above the earth's surface directly over the source and controls. Underground electrodes were used much later using a range of meters where DC field variations and frequencies were recorded. These tests are intriguing and ongoing.

We obtained positive and repeatable results on what can be described as "strong" dowseable natural energy fields. The evidence may suggest these forces are emitted from underground water sources confirmed by water diviners. Guy Underwood thought the most powerful lines were due to underground water lines or aquastats and that animals followed magnetic track lines which influenced the muscles.

Results

The first site revealed source 100 positive ions and 960 negative ions, and over control 1,930 positive ions and 5,049 negative ions. Spectrum readings at peak on source 2,341 Hz – 1,009m/Vac (millivolts) and control 2,445 Hz – 3.798m/Vac. The variations formed the same pattern at other sites with voltage readings and ion counts and also when the same site was tested again during other visits, though of course the readings between sites varied. For example, we may find the source 670 positive ions and control 4,680 positive ions, source 7,270 negative ions and control 5,580 negative ions. However, the overall pattern was that positive ions were consistently lower than controls and there were few exceptions to this rule.

The frequency counter connected to an electrode [lead screened, double insulated] was fed down a small-diameter drilled hole 18 inches (45 centimetres) below ground. An intermittent signal was obtained, at first 10 Hz then with a 6-second delay between each reading 20, 40, reaching 60 Hz, then vanished. We also had to vanish to escape freezing weather and headed for the pub. Will be back!

What are air ions? A brief description

The word *ion*, derived from a Greek verb, suggests *motion*. The term was initially used to describe effects observed when electrical currents were passed through various solutions and caused molecules to migrate to electrodes of opposite polarity. Air ions are defined as atoms that have lost or gained electrons. If an electron is lost the atom becomes positively charged and becomes a positive ion, and gaining an electron makes it a negative ion.

When an atom or molecule has an equal number of electrons and protons it is electrically balanced or neutral. Matter is made of atoms and the Earth's primary forces, electric, nuclear and gravitational.

Ions are present naturally in the air and believed to be made up of 80% radioactive earth elements of which 40% is radon gas, and solar and cosmic radiation equates to 20%. Radon gas forms from the decay of radioactive matter leading to formation of ion pairs. Air ions are created equal and there is no difference between the ions produced by Earth's radioactive materials or cosmic rays. A few hundred feet above the Earth's surface cosmic rays become the source.

Other sources (generally negative ions) arise from triboelectric charges from waterfalls and ocean waves, and are comprised mainly of negatively charged oxygen. The passage of cosmic rays and solar radiation in the upper atmosphere increases during lightning storms and thus dramatically changes the balance of positive and negative ions within the atmosphere. Air ions are again formed when sufficient force displaces an outer electron from a molecule of one of the common gases such as oxygen and nitrogen. When the molecule is left with a positive charge the free electron is picked up by an adjacent molecule which becomes negatively charged.

Pure outdoor air usually contains around 2,000-3,000 ions per cubic centimetre but this is disrupted due to rising pollution levels. In normal conditions there are around five positive ions for every four negative ions. Ions do not live forever but combine with other particles and plate out on surfaces. Small ions (as opposed to large ions) stay around a little longer and attach to oxygen molecules or particles of opposite polarity which are then breathed deep into the lungs.

Pollution levels exist in the atmosphere and inside buildings, in particular where electromagnetic fields are strong. Chemical, electrical, and electrostatic forces all create positive ions. An electrostatic field interacts with the charged air molecules and attract air ions of opposite polarity to the charge that created the field.

The experiments at Avebury and other locations might suggest this energy is caused in part by water forced through narrow underground fissures which perhaps interact with a second stream of water arriving and crossing the same point. Heat, much deeper down, is the likely primary force which also carries electromagnetic forces.

Does gravitation play a part?

Water under atmospheric pressure spins out of the bath tub as one may observe water being forced up in a circular motion from a shallow river bed. Further experiments are needed to find if other dowsed anomalies follow a similar pattern. Underwood suggested that water interacting with certain geological conditions produces electromagnetic spiral formations, and blind springs. Unfortunately such experiments are time consuming and costly.

While using the ion counter at two separate occasions over one strong Geopathic Stress Zone, compared to controls, similar variations to those at Avebury were noted and worth further investigation.

Thank you to David Webb for offering his equipment, time and expertise in analysing dowsable earth energies. His results allow us to understand the phenomena on a scientific level. David's experiments indicate that underground water may produce dowsable 'earth energies' which Guy Underwood always stated. David's academic engineering background and no-nonsense approach has shown that the earth energies recognised by our forebears who marked their presence by standing stones and mounds really do emit tangible energies that can be detected and analysed and I am indebted to David for his contribution and assistance

David specializes in detecting man-made and Geopathic Stress Zones within homes and workspaces and is available for personal consultation. He is especially experienced in working with electro-chemically sensitive people to improve their life styles. David will be able to analyse what is really going on in your home from your WiFi and deck phones signals to your PC or lap top. His experience, wisdom and advice is invaluable.

APPENDIX 4
Earth energy colour essences

Eleven earth colours are used to make the essences: infrared red, orange, yellow, spiritual gold, positive green, blue, indigo, violet, ultraviolet and white. Each essence is made with love over the earth energy point that emits a high frequency and colour ray required to make the remedy. The essences are the energy signature of the vibrations of the Earth captured in water. Each essence comes in a 30ml green glass bottle; green represents the colour of the Earth and the heart chakra.

Removing Blockages essence *Infrared ray* made at Stonehenge. An excellent remedy for removing blockages caused by fear, or even a past-life trauma. With the right light conditions at one of the sarsen stones at Stonehenge it is like looking into a mirror. Its reflective qualities allow you to see inside of yourself, what is blocking your process, whilst giving you an understanding of how to move forward. A powerful remedy that encourages you to go beyond fear with renewed faith, will integrity and inner strength.

Purification essence *Ultraviolet ray* made over the cleansing vortex at Avebury Henge. Prior to entering the Avebury complex one would stand over the cleansing vortex in Avebury's avenue. This remedy clears and cleanses the auric field of unwanted influences.

Transformation essence *Spiritual gold ray* made over the prime meridian ley at Stonehenge. This is an alchemic remedy that helps to bring about transformation. If you wish to change direction in your life, or transform your life, this remedy will prepare you for that journey. The timeless power of Stonehenge offers wisdom and earth magic.

Chakra Balancing essence *Glastonbury Abbey*. Glastonbury Abbey is laid out on an earth energy chakra system. Seven pulsating energy points represent the chakras and cause the Mary energy current to split into two. Five chakra points are in a linear line and two points are offset. The European royal bloodline used these locations to clear, cleanse and encourage the chakra to open. Royal christenings would involve interacting with the seven main points. Today's christenings involve the blessing of the Third Eye chakra with holy water which is ineffective if the other chakras are ignored. This remedy cleanses the chakra system.

Courage essence *Positive red ray* made at Liddington Castle, Wiltshire, which was a Druid stronghold. This sacred landscape gives strength and courage. Upon this hilltop King Arthur fought his twelfth and most famous battle, the Battle of Badon. The energies of Liddington Castle are powerful and give both courage and wisdom combined so that you have the physical energy and insight to succeed. Arthur fought dark forces here and was victorious.

Celestial Vision essence *Blue ray* made at the Druid astronomical earthen enclosure, close to Stonehenge. Standing within this earthen ring on high ground is awe-inspiring. At night you feel so very close to the moon and stars, as if you can touch them! This remedy encourages a celestial vision so take it in the evening, at night or before you go to bed. Attune to higher celestial energies and receive a meaningful vision or dream.

Spiritual Expansion *Spiritual gold ray* made over the Templar Vortex at St Mary's church, Wiltshire. These extraordinary power points within churches and cathedrals were known to expand the aura and give one spiritual insight. This essence appears to do exactly what the power point does, expand your aura. Take the essence and wait for around 5 minutes and then measure the aura and it will have expanded. It increases intuition and deep spiritual understanding. This remedy is also healing.

Healing Essence – Emotional *Green heart chakra ray* made over the geospiral at Avebury. A loving, gentle remedy which soothes and heals emotional issues. It can also help children who have been bullied and blends well with *courage essence* so that the sensitive child (or child within) has the strength to step forward no matter what.

Healing Essence – Release *Harmonic ultraviolet ray* Made at Newgrange in Ireland. A healing remedy that encourages the gentle release of painful memories. It brings hope and a sense of renewed faith that encourages you to move forward. I recommend that you have support, such as friend to call upon, as this remedy will bring stuff up.

Druid Wisdom essence *Blue ray* made at an ancient Druid Cor. Cors were Druid Colleges and one Cor was sited close to Stonehenge (on private ground) where this essence was made. The essence connects you to the Celtic Path, to the Fey and to past Druid Teachers. When I first made this remedy I took it at an old Celtic Cor where it was made. I was looking out at the beautiful vistas and I could see for miles. Suddenly I sensed that I was a part of everything and that everything was a part of me. I lay on the ground and smelt the earth, heard the skylarks above and felt the presence of a Druid Master which inspired me to learn more about magico-aspect of nature. He is still an essential part of my spiritual life and my Druid guide who encouraged me to make these remedies.

Divine Feminine essence *Violet ray* made over the Venus energy vortex at Stanton Drew. It encourages the intuitive faculty to develop for the greater good of all. A loving essence from Gaia which puts you in touch with the Divine feminine within and without.

Beauty Within essence *Orange ray* made within Stoney Littleton long barrow. There are times when we feel like the ugly duckling, when really we are all majestic swans swimming through the sacred river of life. When at a low ebb take this harmonic orange essence to brighten up your day. Let this remedy speak to your heart and show you that you are a beautiful spark of the Divine Flame. And shine beacon bright.

Seer's essence *Indigo ray* made at Casterley Camp, City of the Druids, which represents the planet Jupiter on the Duke ley. On Casterley Camp the Druids gathered to divine the year ahead. This remedy is magical if you want to really attune to tarot cards, astrology or any other divination system. It brings a sense of visual awareness whilst divining and can be used when developing psychic skills.

Psychic Protection essence *Infinite frequency harmonic infra-white* made over a triple primary spiral at Wayland's Smithy long barrow which was once used as an initiation chamber. This powerful remedy protects you from unwanted influences. One legend tells that at Wayland's Smithy the mighty sword Excalibur was forged. Many years ago during a past-life regression it was revealed to me that at Wayland's Smithy long barrow there was once an old wise blacksmith called Caldur. Here under the instruction of a Druid Magician three swords were forged: Excalibur, of strong steel for the true King of England, and *two other swords*, one of silver and one of gold which preceded Excalibur. The Silver Sword was made for a Celtic Queen which represented feminine strength, lunar vision and a fair and just heart. The Gold Sword was the sword of True Wealth – wisdom, health and solar light. At one time the swords were united and stuck into the ground upon the long barrow. One stood upright and the other two were placed in the ground at a slight angle creating the Druid Yod, a symbol representing the three rays of divine light. At Beltane (May 1st) the Gold Sword was taken to Mayfair in London (for Beltane fertility and wealth rites, hence its name of 'May') and here it remains buried amid the wealthiest part of London. This essence has the protective power of all three swords shielding you from harm as long as you are a true servant of Gaia, Great Spirit and humanity.

The essences will be added to each year, so please look at the website for more details. www.theaveburyexperience.co.uk

The Avebury School of Esoteric Studies
– professional certificated courses

The Avebury School of Esoteric Studies was founded by Maria Wheatley. Maria has been a professional tutor for over 20 years working for the Wiltshire Education Authority, England, and she has written diploma courses for various private colleges. The Avebury School of Esoteric Studies is affiliated with the **Association of British Correspondence Colleges** and the school offers practical workshops, on-line lessons/webiners, personal SKYPE lessons, CD-Rom home study packages or a traditional hardback manual.

Dowsing Courses

Dowsing professionally is a practical two-day certificated dowsing course, or a home study correspondence course. The comprehensive home study course contains 12 lessons which are emailed in two sections, Part I and Part II, it is also available on CD-Rom or it can be posted in an A4 manual format. Alternatively, you can choose Personal Skype Lessons. Six one-hour Skype tutorials combined with home study lessons are particularly popular, as this style of learning offers the student personal and expert teaching to support distant learning. Making learning simple with practical and visual learning tools, Maria offers videos of how to dowse, so that you can see how a particular dowsing task can be achieved on her YouTube Channel.

Synopsis of the course

Day 1 of the practical course, or Part I of the home study course

Introduction to dowsing

We will explore the history of dowsing from ancient China to the present day. What dowsing is and why anyone can do it! We will experiment with different dowsing instruments and discuss what causes the dowsing reaction from the 'sixth sense' to brain wave activity influencing the muscles and how the lunar phases influence our dowsing sensitivity.

Developing mental dowsing principles – 'frame of mind' and visualization

Simple mental principles, such as relaxed concentration, 'frame of mind' and visualization are the key tools of successful dowsing. Students will gain a full understanding and in-depth awareness of the various mental disciplines required for successful dowsing and easy to follow exercises which encourage the discipline to develop.

Developing physical dowsing skills – rod handling and how to hold a pendulum

Fundamental dowsing skills are explored in detail so that you can master the key principles of dowsing such as:

- How to handle the rods and pendulum correctly.
- How to check that you are 'in balance' before you begin a dowsing session. If you are out of balance, you cannot dowse efficiently resulting in incorrect answers.

Rod programming

- How to establish 'yes' and 'no' responses.
- How to recognise false or trick answers.
- What causes false or trick answers.

Information dowsing

How (and when) to ask the rods or pendulum a question is examined in detail.

Directional dowsing and the 'Show me technique'

Directional dowsing is an important dowsing skill which allows one to detect and locate large objects, such as a nearby church or school, to smaller objects in the home. Using this key skill, visible objects can be found, and with practise, this skill will become second nature and you will be able to find invisible targets such as earth energies. Several practical exercises are given which encourage the student to put the theory into practise and test their newly found skill.

Establishing an accuracy reference point

Another fundamental and key divining skill which determines the exact location of a dowsing target.

The essential art of tracking

The ability to follow or track water and gas pipes, telecommunication cabling, and sewer pipes is demonstrated and explained. This skill can also be applied to locate and track global grid systems, geopathic stress zones, leys, earth energies, and underground streams. Students will gain a practical understanding of tracking by following easy and fun exercises.

Remanence dowsing

How to trace the etheric outline of an object long gone, or how to follow the invisible trail of someone's steps when they are not insight is easy to master by following simple precepts.

Map dowsing

Using a pendulum to locate places, peoples, or substances in relation to a map. Home study only.

Nature and dowsing

Certain plants and animals are attracted by certain energies such as underground water, geopathic stress zones and earth energies. We will learn how to use nature to identify the location and presence of certain energies.

Day 2 of the practical course, or Part II of the home study course

Health and Well Being

In this section we will explore how to use dowsing to enhance our health and well-being and to locate the major harmonic surface patterns that the earth emits. Living in harmony with the earth is a fundamental part of this course and also learning how to identify some of the earth's most powerful energies is an essential aspect of being a professional geomancer.

Aura detection and chakra balancing

Using a pendulum to ascertain if the chakras are in balance and how to rebalance, activate, or calm chakras. We will also learn how to dowse and cleanse an aura using colour.

Activating the earthstar chakra

Using mediation we will activate the earthstar chakra which is positioned just beneath your feet. Once this chakra is opened it creates a bridge between you and Gaia and heighten your awareness of earth energies.

Dowsing toxic grids

There are grid systems which cover the planet from pole to pole, like a gigantic fish net. The lines and some of the crossing points are especially toxic to live above. We will learn to detect the toxic grids and the locations which emit geopathic stress.

- The first global grid system can have an adverse influence in the home or workplace.
- The second global grid system – the Curry net has a very harmful influence.
- The Benker grid system is harmful to living organisms.
- Evidence for the grids and how to negate their influence.

A chakra grid cross

If a person has interacted with negative energy or geopathic stress, a distinctive pattern emanates from the chakra system. We will learn how to recognise a positive chakra pattern and a negative chakra pattern and how to re-balance the former so that the chakra system functions harmoniously. This is an important aspect of health dowsing.

Locating positive and negative energies within a house, workspace or landscape is essential. This section of the course will focus on the most powerful forms of earth energy.

- **Pattern recognition** all energy lines and patterns can be easily recognized by their harmonic surface pattern. We will learn to identify the following energies which emit distinctive patterns. An expert dowser will instantly be aware of the type of energy found and one way to achieve this is to apply pattern recognition.

- **The geospiral** is the surface pattern of underground yin water which is all healing.

- **The harmonic crossing points** of yin streams, the healing pattern it emits, and its healing field.

- **The stream band** is the harmonic surface pattern of an underground stream flowing predominantly with yang water, which is injurious to health.

- **The crossing point of yang streams** and the toxic pattern it emits. A distinctive pattern that once dictated the placement of ancient gallows and sites of execution. Areas upon the earth which bring out feelings of foreboding and attract hauntings.

- **Earth chimneys** are high-energy points that occur every 32 feet (10 metres). We will experience how they were integrated into ancient sites, European churches and cathedrals.

- **Earth springs** or power points these are energetic locations which have an outpouring of negative ions which are conducive to good health; but not favourable to live above.

- **Harmonizing negative areas and leys** some dowsers suggest that you should move a negative ley. However, if you have a cold and the symptoms are a runny nose, I don't move your nose! So why move Gaia's energy lines? By doing so, you are simply transferring the negative energy elsewhere and this is not good practice. Sensitive dowsers raise the energy level of a line or earth current but only where necessary as some life forms thrive above such lines and I will demonstrate how this is achieved.

High standards are required alongside dowsing tasks and homework sessions. Upon successful completion you will be awarded a certificate, which will enable you to become insured as a professional dowser.

Testimonial Dr Jude Currivan, cosmologist, healer and author of HOPE
In the mid 1990s I was very fortunate to be introduced to and guided in the art of dowsing by the great master dowser Dennis Wheatley. Dennis's enormous knowledge, straight-forward approach, easy companionship and willingness to answer all my questions(!) made him the perfect teacher. I'm delighted that his daughter Maria now continues the family tradition of sharing this wonderfully valuable art and science with the world.

Professional Dowsing advanced level
Master Practitioner certificated course

Divining the Earth

The most comprehensive course on earth energies, leys and grid lines in the UK. Study this course in two practical workshops, or with a home study package, on line, or SKYPE lessons.

The course has two sections.

- Level I Earth energies and leys.
- Level II The Healing and Shadow Grid Lines.

Some knowledge of dowsing is necessary prior to this course. However, two Skype lessons will cover the dowsing skills required to participate.

Synopsis of the course

Day One of the practical course or Part 1 of the home study course

Explore the powerful earth energies and grid lines which interlace the planet, some of which are featured in this book. Learn how to identify, harmonize and interpret the land. Maria is considered a leading authority on the geodetic system of earth energies and she can share her knowledge and deep understanding of the Gaia's energies with you.

- Locate healing patterns, holy lines, and geodetic power centres.
- Leys, ley systems, and dragon lines - how to find and interpret them.
- Genesis lines, interacting with this powerful energy, and following its serpentine path.
- Identifying the geodetic system of earth energies. The geospiral, primary and secondary haloes, and energy arcs. We will explore in detail the harmonic healing properties of water and how the geospiral pattern and

its many different sized coils represent the chakra system. For example, a three and a half coiled geospiral represents the base chakra and a 7-coiled geospiral represents the heart chakra.

- The geodetic system of earth energies of the water line, aquastat and track lines.
- How to recognize how geodetic lines flow through the earth.
- Colour Dowsing and the meaning of the 12 earth colours.
- How the earth colours influence the land and the aura.
- Learn how to make colour healing earth energy essences and harmonic healing water.
- Colour healing the land – applying the earth colours to heal and negate toxic and stagnant energies.
- Attuning to your Vivaxis – the magnetic aspect of your being.

Day Two of the practical course or Part II of the home study course

Level II The Healing Grids and the Shadow Grids

German research shows that the Earth is surrounded by seven major grids, each of which is associated with a planet and a chakra. These grids are harmonic as they can enhance our ability to communicate, heal us, or they can be used to resolve karmic issues. Discover how to locate these lines of force and tap into the power lines, as did our ancient forebears, the Knights Templar and the Masonic Brotherhood.

There are also 'shadow' grids, which are the mirror image of the positive grids and they flow in the opposite direction. They cover the planet from pole from pole and they are especially injurious as they induce paranoia, mental fatigue, and fear and should be avoided or harmonized. Discover how to locate the grids using a compass and a dowsing rod.

This fascinating course puts you in touch with Gaia and features the teachings of the Master Dowsers, Guy Underwood and Dennis and Maria Wheatley. After studying this course you will become a **Master Practitioner of Dowsing** with exceptional ability to attune to the Earth Force and interpret its invisible flows and frequencies.

This Master Practitioner course is not taught anywhere else in the UK and is the result of over 70 years of combined research. Expert tuition alongside practical exercises will give you a deep understanding of the land upon which you live.

Other certificated courses:

Earth Divination – the ancient art of geomancy

Earth divination or geomancy is one of the oldest divination systems which was originally devised by shaman to commune with the Earth. Millennia ago, when facing uncertainty, or seeking advise, a shaman would throw sacred seeds upon the Earth and the pattern or position they created would be interpreted. Earth divination consists of sixteen sacred earth symbols which represent a force of nature or one of Gaia's seasons or expressions. Collectively, the sixteen geomantic symbols were understood to be the silent language of Mother Earth. When consulting the symbols you are talking to the Earth Mother. Alternatively, pebbles or stones were often cast upon the earth and this ancient tradition was developed and revered by the ancient priesthood. There are eight *power symbols* which can be used to heal the earth, change a mood or aid manifestation and their energies are powerful yet very gentle and loving. Maria has been working with the symbols of Mother Earth for over 20 years and will share her experience and knowledge with you. Home study and Skype lessons are now available.

Earth divination is very diverse from reading the future to cleansing a house these ancient symbols born of the Earth are truly divine.

Tarot Reading Made Easy. Skype or practical workshops only.

I was taught how to read tarot cards when I was 16 by two Romanies. They showed me how to learn ten cards at once by learning the song or story of each of the four suits. I have successfully taught hundreds of people how to read the cards and they were amazed at how fast they could learn this ancient art.

Past Life Regression Level I and II.

A great course that is comprehensive and will give you the key skills to safely use regression. I have been teaching this subject since 1996.

Maria also leads dowsing tours of sacred sites in the UK, Scotland, Ireland and Brittany.

For more information: **www.theaveburyexperience.co.uk**

mariawheatley@aol.com